WHEAT-FREE
GLUTEN-FREE

Wheat-Free Gluten-Free

200 Delicious Dishes to Make Eating a Pleasure

• •

Michelle Berriedale-Johnson

Foreword by Dr. Stefano Guandalini, M.D.

SURREY BOOKS • CHICAGO

Wheat-Free Gluten-Free
is published by Surrey Books, Inc.,
230 E. Ohio St., Suite 120, Chicago, IL 60611.

First U.S. edition: 2 3 4 5
(First published by Grub Street, London, England.)

This book is manufactured in the United States of America.

Library of Congress Cataloging-in-Publication Data

Berriedale-Johnson, Michelle.
  Wheat-free gluten-free : 200 delicious dishes to make eating a pleasure /
Michelle Berriedale-Johnson. — 1st U.S. ed.
      p. cm.
Includes index.
  ISBN 1-57284-045-5 (trade paper)
1. Gluten-free diet—Recipes. 2. Wheat-free diet—Recipes. 3. Celiac
disease—Diet therapy—Recipes. I. Title: Wheat free gluten free. II. Title.
  RM237.86 .B475 2002
  641.5'63—dc21

                                                              2002004885

Distributed to the trade by Publishers Group West.

Contents

Foreword

I clearly remember the very first child I saw with celiac disease, when I was a student in medical school over thirty years ago. This young child had all of the "classic" symptoms of celiac disease commonly seen in my home country of Italy— a bloated stomach, knobby knees and elbows, thin arms and legs, pale skin and many bouts of diarrhea. As I examined this frail child, I knew that I would dedicate my medical career to helping children and families affected by celiac disease.

As a pediatric gastroenterologist, I have diagnosed hundreds of children with celiac disease, conducted numerous research studies on the condition, published many research papers and authored the guidelines most commonly used by physicians around the world.

As a physician in Italy, I worked in a medical system that routinely screened young children for celiac disease, and with colleagues in adult medicine who would test adults for the condition at the first sign of symptoms. As a result, the average time to diagnosis for people with celiac disease in Italy is only a few weeks to a few months.

Despite my training and experience as a physician and researcher, I was unprepared for the situation I found when I came to work in the United States. I kept asking myself one question: Where are the children with celiac disease?

Research on the rates of celiac disease in the U.S. clearly show that it is as common here as it is in Europe, affecting 1 in 169 healthy, average Americans. Yet we also know that roughly 1 in 8,000 Americans is actually diagnosed with the disease. This is truly a crisis, yet most U.S. physicians receive less than 20 minutes of instruction on celiac disease throughout their years in medical school. The average length of time it takes for a child to be diagnosed in the U.S. is two years; for adults that span increases to ten years.

It is also well established that a delayed diagnosis of celiac disease predisposes children and adults to autoimmune disorders, and neurological conditions like epilepsy, bone problems such as osteoporosis, learning difficulties, short stature, delayed puberty and infertility, and even cancer.

Complicating this situation is the fact that celiac disease may manifest itself very differently in Americans, as compared to Europeans. There are 256 signs and symptoms related to celiac disease as it appears in children and adults in the U.S., and in many cases, these symptoms first appear unrelated and can be somewhat mild. The most obvious difference is the paucity of GI symptoms in the U.S. The damage caused by the disease, however, is often unrelated to the severity of the symptoms.

Once diagnosed, people with celiac disease often receive little information or guidance about the only treatment for celiac disease: the gluten-free diet. As a result, some celiacs may feel that they cannot have certain dishes (even though they can be prepared gluten-free) or that they are not able to enjoy foods anymore, as the diet seems restrictive. In addition, some people with celiac disease are not told that the diet is a lifelong treatment for the condition, and they mistakenly stop eating gluten-free foods after a couple of years.

A coordinated effort involving scientific research, medical education, public awareness and patient services is required in order to improve diagnosis rates and improve the quality of life for people who are diagnosed with celiac disease in this country. That's why I've created the University of Chicago Celiac Disease Program, which aims to increase diagnosis rates for celiac disease and ensure that newly diagnosed celiacs receive guidance about the gluten-free diet. In only a few years, we have been able to make a substantial impact on these important issues. We are proud to work with the support groups and patient organizations that have faithfully served the celiac community for years; we work with them to effect change for the future.

WHAT IS CELIAC DISEASE?

Celiac disease is an autoimmune disorder, which is to say that it is not an allergy. The difference is that in celiac disease, the body attacks itself—the small intestine—when gluten is eaten and digested. (In an allergy, the immune system causes symptoms as a result of an allergen, but the immune system does not actually damage tissues of the body.) It is important to understand the difference because many of the long-term effects of untreated celiac disease occur as a result of the damage that is caused.

Celiac disease is also genetic, where a certain type of genetic material, called HLA, is passed on from parent to child at the time of conception. Individuals who inherit a certain type of HLA from their parents have a predisposition to developing celiac disease. Individuals who do not have this genetic material will not develop celiac disease. There is an HLA test for celiac disease that will determine which members of a celiac's family should be monitored for celiac disease.

Gluten, a protein found in wheat, rye and barley, is the trigger for an autoimmune reaction in people with celiac disease. When gluten reaches the small intestine, the body's immune system does not recognize it as a part of food. Instead it mounts an attack against the gluten, thinking of it as an invader that should be destroyed. However, this attack sets off a chain of events that results in inflammation, damaging the tissue (villi) of the intestinal wall. These villi are important; they absorb the beneficial nutrients, vitamins, and minerals from food. When they are damaged, the body cannot use these nutrients. When gluten is removed from the diet in people with celiac disease, the intestine repairs itself and the villi function normally.

Dermatitis Herpetiformis (DH) is a skin manifestation of celiac disease. It is an itchy rash that appears on the knees, elbows and buttocks, and it is treated with the gluten-free diet and a cream called Dapsone. This rash will always be located on both sides of the body, which helps to distinguish it from other skin conditions.

HOW IS CELIAC DISEASE DIAGNOSED?

There are several steps to the diagnosis of celiac disease, and it is important that each step is followed in order to establish a clear diagnosis. It is also important not to begin the gluten-free diet until a diagnosis is reached. The tests and procedures used to diagnose celiac disease will not be accurate if an individual is on a gluten-free diet.

Antibody Testing: There are several antibody tests that will measure the level of immune response in the blood stream. These tests can only indicate if further investigation into celiac disease is warranted; they do not diagnose celiac disease.

Endoscopic Biopsy: This is a test performed by a gastroenterologist, and it is done on an outpatient basis. After numbing the patient's throat (for adults) or the administration of anesthesia (for children), the physician will insert a small fiber-optic tube down the throat, through the stomach and into the small intestine. A small camera on the tube allows photographs to be taken at any point in the procedure and guides the physician as biopsy samples are taken. Usually 4-6 samples, taken from different areas of the duodenum, are needed to diagnose celiac disease. The entire procedure takes less than 20 minutes and does not cause pain. The biopsy results will conclusively establish celiac disease.

Introduction of the Gluten-Free Diet: The final "test" is the introduction of the gluten-free diet and measuring a patient's response to the diet at 6-12 month intervals. If symptoms improve, antibody levels drop and other clinical factors improve, the diagnosis is confirmed.

WHAT IS THE GLUTEN-FREE DIET?

Gluten is a protein found in wheat, rye and barley. Food products can contain these grains or flours made from them, such as bread, pasta or blue cheese. In addition, many food additives are made from these grains, like barley malt. (It was commonly, but mistakenly, thought that gluten was also found in oats, but this is not the case.)

The gluten-free diet is a lifelong enterprise, one that requires the newly diagnosed celiac and his/her family to research the content of foods, experiment by adapting recipes, and find support from other celiacs. In fact, these days it is possible to find delicious replacements for menu standbys like pasta or bread, or to make that family recipe with a special blend of gluten-free flours. This gluten-free cookbook is a key to unlocking the door to interesting, healthy and delicious meals for people with celiac disease.

There are a few guidelines that will help any celiac eliminate gluten from his or her diet:

- Food labels do not, as yet, refer to gluten. Know the numerous ingredient names that contain gluten and the other terms that mean gluten is in a product.
- Call manufacturers to ask how their products are made. Remember that a gluten-free product that comes in contact with a food that contains gluten can cause symptoms in people with celiac disease.
- Prevent contamination of gluten-free foods by using a dedicated toaster and by using utensils carefully when preparing foods. If you are spreading butter on the family's toast for Sunday morning breakfast and stick a knife in the butter and then put it on gluten-containing bread, the knife, when put back in the butter container, will bring with it crumbs from the bread. If the next person's toast is gluten-free, those crumbs are now spread on it with the butter.

It is also important to avoid non-food items that contain gluten that could be ingested (swallowed in some way). For children, play-dough can be a culprit as it is usually made of wheat flour (alternative recipes are available). Cosmetics and lotions should be researched, and toothpaste should be gluten-free. Note that it is important to ask your physician to prescribe non-gluten containing medications.

PREGNANCY

It is a common misconception that the gluten-free diet is not good for a developing fetus. In fact, research shows that women with celiac disease who are not on a gluten-free diet are more likely to suffer a miscarriage or develop anemia during the pregnancy. The gluten-free diet has all of the nutrients that a person or fetus needs to grow and thrive, and a woman who wants to ensure a healthy pregnancy should maintain her gluten-free diet throughout.

There are many resources available to the newly diagnosed celiac that will provide a more in-depth view of the gluten-free diet. In addition, the American Dietetic Association has recently updated their guidelines on the gluten-free diet. These guidelines are available to dietitians across the country. Please use the resource section at the back of this book for more information and guidance.

— Stefano Guandalini, M.D.
  Section Chief, Pediatrics Gastroenterology, Hepatology and Nutrition
   University of Chicago Children's Hospital
  Director, University of Chicago Celiac Disease Program

Introduction

Even if you only read the occasional women's magazine, you cannot have failed to notice that it has at least one article in every issue on food-related health. It could be about an allergy or it could be about food related to depression or to asthma or to arthritis or to your child's failure to do well at school—or to almost anything else!

But why this obsession with food? Well, the proposition that "we are what we eat" seems a fairly reasonable one to most people. But what are we eating? Food scandals over the last few years have become more and more frequent. The salmonella and eggs scandal; mad cow disease; E-coli poisoning from cooked meats. And what about the genetic modification of our food? Or the pesticide residues which were recently so high that we were advised to peel our carrots so as to avoid eating the pesticides left on the surface ? Or the antibiotics fed so regularly to animals that they are no longer effective when used to treat humans?

And those are only the food scandals that hit the headlines. Sophisticated, highly technical food manufacturing and plant breeding techniques over the last fifty years have changed our food almost beyond recognition. More importantly, they have caused nearly all the food we eat to be processed many times, subject to violent changes in temperature, while its ingredients have had their chemical structures altered to achieve what are thought to be better textures or better tastes.

As yet we really do not know exactly what effects these changes have had on our bodies. But we do know that they have come extremely quickly (in fifty years) and that animals (including humans) evolve very slowly—over thousands of years. So there is a good chance that our bodies may have a problem coping with such dramatic changes.

As far as the subject of this book is concerned—wheat and gluten allergy or intolerance—this rapid change is very relevant.

Gluten, found primarily in wheat, is a gluey substance which is enormously useful to food manufacturers as it does, literally, glue or bind ingredients together. Gluten holds together the flour which makes bread, for example, when the yeast expands to make the bread dough rise. Gluten stops sauces or soups from curdling while it gives a smooth texture to cheese spread and dips, dressings, margarines, sweets, canned meats, mustard and a thousand other products on the supermarket shelves. It has therefore been in the manufacturers' interests to use it extensively and in the growers' interests to increase the gluten content of grains.

Some medical practitioners see gluten as one of the main trouble makers in the modern diet. Because it is a type of protein, the body tries to absorb it in the same way that it absorbs other nutrition-bearing proteins. But, unfortunately, not only is gluten entirely lacking in nutrition itself, but because of its natural stickiness it can clog up our guts and move, undigested, into our bloodstreams.

For celiacs gluten presents a particular problem as it damages the internal lining of their digestive tracts. For wheat intolerants the situation is slightly different as there is no certainty as to which constituent of the wheat is upsetting them—or maybe it is no particular constituent but the combination of individual elements which make up the wheat grain.

The conditions of celiac disease and wheat intolerance are often confused as the symptoms of, and treatment for, both conditions are very similar. As an added complication, the symptoms for both vary enormously and the longer patients remain undiagnosed, the sicker they are likely to become and the more varied their symptoms are likely to be!

The most obvious of these symptoms are usually digestive and run as follows:

- Diarrhea (and occasionally constipation)
- Bloating
- Abdominal pain
- Flatulence
- Nausea and vomiting.

However, there is another batch of common symptoms common to both conditions which do not relate to the digestion:

- Chronic fatigue
- Weight loss
- Lactose intolerance
- Bone pain
- Depression.

Psychological problems are not uncommon.
And, as if that were not enough:

- Headaches
- Mouth ulcers
- Asthma
- Fainting and chest pains—have all also been caused by wheat intolerance.

In babies and small children there are other indications, especially of celiac disease. These are:

- General failure to thrive
- Diarrhea
- Bloating
- Vomiting
- Fatty and smelly stools.

There is also an increasing amount of evidence to suggest that wheat intolerance could be very important in childhood psychological disorders such as hyperactivity and autism.

CELIAC DISEASE

Celiac disease is not, medically speaking, an intolerance or allergy but an autoimmune disease. It can occur in babies, children or adults and is a state in which that person's immune system reacts against a specific substance that they touch, breathe or, in the case of celiac disease, eat.

In a celiac's case the immune system reacts against the protein called gluten found in wheat, rye, barley and possibly oats. The gluten damages the lining of the small intestine.

A normal small intestine is covered with tiny fingerlike fronds or protrusions called villi which absorb nutrients from food. In celiac disease one element of the protein gluten (called gliadin) damages the villi so badly that they are flattened into little humps and are unable to absorb nutrients at all. This is why untreated celiacs, apart from their other symptoms, will continue to lose weight. In most cases, as soon as gluten is removed from the diet the villi recover and continue to behave as normal. If the condition remains untreated for a long time, however, the villi may be so badly damaged that they will never entirely recover their full function.

HISTORY

The Roman physician, Galen, described a condition in which the digestion was upset by farinaceous foods (foods containing gluten) as early as the second century B.C. In the 19th century carbohydrates (including gluten-bearing farinaceous food) in general were thought to be the problem. In fact, it is possible that total carbohydrate intolerance may still be a problem for the relatively small number of people who do not get well when they stop eating gluten.

Nineteenth century patients were put on a no-carbohydrate, high-fat diet—a terribly difficult diet to follow! Matters improved when, in the 1920s two American doctors discovered that their patients could eat bananas and banana flour (even though bananas are very high in carbohydrates) without becoming ill.

However, it was the terrible food shortages suffered by the Dutch during the second world war that pointed the finger at gluten rather than total carbohydrates. For a long period during the war there was no regular gluten bread to be had in Holland—and celiacs all over the country got better!

By the 1950s new biopsy techniques allowed doctors to remove a sample from the small intestine so that they could examine the gluten-flattened villi in detail. This made diagnosis relatively straightforward.

TREATMENT

Once you have been diagnosed as a celiac the treatment is simple—stay off gluten. This may sound easy but it is not, mainly because of the very widespread use of gluten in food processing that I talked about earlier. However, it is very important that if you are a celiac you do keep rigidly to your gluten-free diet as your body, especially if you have suffered from the condition for a long time before diagnosis, will be extremely sensitive and will react to the tiniest amount of gluten with a dramatic return of your symptoms.

If, as a diagnosed celiac, you do not improve on a gluten-free diet, then it is worth looking into other food sensitivities (dairy, soy, fish or almost any food you eat regularly). If your gut lining (the tissue on the inside of your intestine) was badly damaged before you were diagnosed it may still be "leaky," allowing other food molecules, to which you may be sensitive, into your bloodstream. If your body is low in zinc this can make the problem worse.

THE OAT QUESTION

Gluten is found in most grains (wheat, barley, rye and oats—though not rice) so grain is effectively off the menu for celiacs. There is, however, a query over oats. Although oats are a grain they do not contain gliadin but a gliadin analogue (an identikit gliadin) called avelin, and it is not certain whether or not this actually affects celiacs. Medical trials carried out in Finland suggest that it does not, but these trials are not comprehensive. Nor are doctors sure whether, although celiacs may show no immediate reaction to avelin, it might do them some long-term damage. Medical advice therefore is to be extremely careful: if you are badly affected by celiac disease, or are elderly or a child, it is probably wiser to take no risks and stay off oats as well as the other grains.

DERMATITIS HERPETIFORMIS

There is a fairly rare form of dermatitis called Dermatitis Herpetiformis, whose symptoms are itchy patches on the elbows and behind the knees, followed by the lower back and other parts of the body. This is also caused by damaged villi and its treatment is exactly the same as for celiac disease—no gluten.

WHEAT INTOLERANCE
Wheat intolerance falls into a quite separate medical compartment from celiac disease as it is a food intolerance rather than an auto-immune condition. Essentially this means that you should be able to recover from it although there are a few people who are so badly affected that they will need to remain wheat-free for good.

WHY DO FOOD INTOLERANCES OCCUR?
There are no definite answers as to why people develop food intolerances although it seems clear that over-indulgence combined with a depressed immune system is usually at least part of the cause. Nationally, people tend to be most intolerant to the foods they eat most. In northern Europe the main intolerances are to dairy products and wheat; in North America to corn; in the Far East to soy and so on.

It also seems pretty clear that a healthy person can eat most foods without a problem but if they stop being healthy—they suffer a gastro-intestinal or viral illness, are involved in an accident of some kind, suffer a bereavement or family break-up, are overworked, over-tired, or overstressed, are not properly nourished (in terms of vitamins, minerals—not calories!) and so on—their bodies become less able to cope. At that point they may react badly to foods which under normal circumstances they could eat with no problems.

In medical terms, this could be because they are no longer producing the correct amount or type of enzymes needed to break down and digest the food. Food may not therefore be properly "processed" before it enters the bloodstream. It is also possible that as a result of their illness the lining of their gut or intestines may have become "leaky" thus allowing undigested proteins into the bloodstream and thereby setting up allergic reactions.

As regards wheat in particular, there are two theories as to why we should react to an excess. One is that humans are omnivores, designed to eat a wide variety of foods, but that the diet of the late 20th century has come to rely far too greatly on wheat and the by-products of wheat.

The other is the "hunter-gatherer" theory which says that our bodies are basically designed to eat meat (hunted) and wild fruits and nuts (gathered). Although we became domesticated some 10,000 odd years ago when we settled down and started to cultivate grains, in evolutionary terms this is no time at all and our systems have just not yet gotten used to this new grain-based diet.

PREVALENCE OF WHEAT AND WHEAT BY-PRODUCTS IN OUR DIETS
Whichever—if either—is right there is no doubt that wheat and wheat by-products (wheat starch and gluten) have all but taken over our diets. Popular Western type food, which is rapidly displacing many traditional Third World diets, depends largely on wheat bread, wheat-based pastas and pizzas, wheat-based biscuits and cakes—and those are only the products where the wheat content is obvious.

As I said earlier, the gluey, elastic substance, or gluten, which is left after the starch in wheat flour is washed away, is enormously useful in the general processing and manufacture of food.

TREATMENT
Someone who is wheat intolerant may be reacting to the gluten in wheat or to some other protein but as with celiac disease, the primary treatment for wheat intolerance is to stop eating wheat! If your digestion (or indeed any part of your body) is under stress, constantly making it do things—or eat things—which it finds difficult, it is only going to put it under yet more stress.

Stopping those stressful behaviors—or not eating those stress-creating foods—even if only for a short while, will give the body a break and a chance to rebuild its own strength. You can help it with plenty of rest, lots of good nutritious food that it can tolerate and reducing any other stresses that may be under your control. Once your general health has improved, you can start gradually reintroducing the problem foods, and there is a good chance that they will be perfectly well tolerated. However, even if you make a total recovery it would be wise to limit your intake of wheat—or whatever food proved to cause sensitivity—in the future to avoid getting into an "overload" situation again.

DIAGNOSIS

If you suspect that you may be suffering from a wheat or gluten intolerance your first port of call should be your general practitioner. Because celiac disease is well recognized, if your symptoms fall within the list on page 2 your doctor may refer you to a gastroenterologist who will perform the normal tests for celiac disease (physical examination, medical history, blood samples, etc.), ending up with a biopsy. However, you would do well to read up on the subject yourself so that you are able to ask the right questions of both your doctor and specialist.

But although you may be reacting to wheat you may not be a celiac, which is good news for you as it means both that your diet will not be quite so restricted, and you probably will get better. However, because food intolerance in general is a relatively uncharted territory as far as most physicians are concerned, you may have more difficulty convincing him or her that wheat could be your problem. If so you might want to visit either your local community dietitian (check with your doctor or your local hospital) or a qualified nutritionist.

Whatever you do, do NOT set off on any kind of exclusion diet without qualified medical advice. This is especially important if you are dealing with a child, an elderly person or anyone who is already on medication or suffers from some other health problem. *It is particularly important when dealing with a possible food allergy or intolerance that one maintain a balanced and varied diet,* and to achieve this when you are cutting out a large swathe of what you normally eat will require experienced professional advice.

REVIEWING YOUR LIFESTYLE

What you can do for yourself is to review your lifestyle. There are, no doubt, a few people who maintain an ideal regimen. They make time for exercise and relaxation, minimize their stress levels through meditation or long walks with the dog, eat a good balanced diet at the right time—and do not overdose on caffeine or red wine! But most of us fall down in some area. And if we get ill and overstressed, far from taking more care of ourselves, all too often we drive ourselves even harder to compensate for our perceived inefficiencies—thus making the whole situation worse.

It is not unheard of for allergy and intolerance problems to disappear all by themselves when the person concerned makes serious changes in lifestyle and allows himself or herself a bit of that "tender loving care" so many shower on others.

MANAGING YOUR FOOD INTAKE

The other thing that wheat intolerants and celiacs will undoubtedly have to do, once they have figured out a sensible diet to pursue, is to take responsibility for their own food. This may sound like an odd thing to say, but the arrival of convenience food on the shelves has meant that we really do not need to think about what we eat at all. If the picture on the pack looks good we take it home, pop it in the microwave—and eat. But that is no good if you are on what effectively is an exclusion diet.

READING THE LABELS

For a start you will need to learn to recognize your gastronomic *bête noir*—and this may not be that easy. Gluten, wheat starch and their derivatives are extremely widely used in the food industry but they are rarely labeled as "Wheat—beware." However, supermarkets are becoming increasingly aware of food intolerance problems and several now highlight potentially allergenic ingredients on their own labels.

Breads, cakes and cookies are obviously a no-no area—but be careful of breads apparently made of other ingredients such as rye (fine for wheat intolerants, no good for celiacs) as they may well contain wheat flour as well. Always read the label with care before buying.

However, your reading cannot stop there, as the most unlikely foods such as salt or mustard may contain wheat by-products. Moreover, you need to know what you are looking for, as it is not always obvious. Below is a list of wheat and gluten derivatives, plus unexpected foods where you may, though not always, find them.

- Alcohol made from grains—beer, whisky, Scotch and most liqueurs
- Barley
- Biscotti
- Bran
- Canned meat containing preservatives
- Canned vegetables unless canned in water only
- Cereal
- Cheese spread and dips
- Chewing gum
- Couscous
- Curry powder
- Farina
- Fruit drinks
- Horseradish creams/sauces
- Instant hot drinks—coffee, tea, chocolate
- Ketchups
- Luncheon or other prepared meats
- Malt
- Margarines
- Monosodium Glutamate
- Mustards
- Oats
- Rye
- Salad dressings—avoid all commercial varieties unless you're sure they are gluten/wheat free
- Sauces—most commercially made sauces or sauce mixes
- Sausages
- Seasoning mixes
- Semolina
- Soups—most commercially made canned or frozen soups
- Soy sauce and most other Chinese sauces, except those marked wheat free
- Starch
- Sweets—any sweets that contain grains and any that contain stabilizers made from gluten
- Wheat flour
- White pepper

Then you have the problem of foods which are not labeled at all—the succulent sausages in the meat department, or the coated cod fillets in the fish section. The sausages will probably contain breadcrumbs, and the fish will be coated in batter or breadcrumbs—both off the menu. So if there is no label you must ask—and not be satisfied with a vague answer. For example you must make sure that the butcher claiming to make gluten-free sausages really does understand about possible contamination with other wheat or gluten products.

If your exclusion diet is to work and you are to get better you must be rigorous. Especially in the early stages when you are still very sensitive (and possibly always for celiacs) you will react strongly to a tiny amount of wheat or gluten, which will not only make you feel awful but set back your recovery.

THE REVIVAL OF HOME COOKERY
The result of all this is that you will inevitably have to make by far the greater part of your food yourself at home. Gone are the days of the convenience pack. The up side to this is that you will probably be eating much healthier and tastier food—and that you may really enjoy cooking!

This may sound fine to someone who is a good and interested cook, but like a nightmare to someone who has difficulty in heating the baked beans without burning them. But things will improve.

Cooking is not some magic art but a very practical and logical skill, quite easily acquired, especially if you have a vested interest in the end result tasting good!

Some foods are very easy to adapt to a gluten or wheat-free diet—potato flour, for example, is just as good a thickener for any kind of sauce or custard (some people would say better) as wheat flour. Other areas are really quite difficult. It is just not possible to produce the equivalent of an ordinary store-bought loaf of white bread, without gluten. One can bake bread, and very nice bread too, but it will be different bread.

Not that this is necessarily a bad thing. There is a strong chance that the reason that you ended up with a wheat intolerance or even celiac disease is because you ate a good deal too much wheat and wheat by-products in the first place. So a good way to ensure that you do not do so again is to broaden your tastes. Then, even if you are able to reintroduce wheat to your diet, you will, by choice, eat less of it.

BUYING GOOD INGREDIENTS
The ingredients that you can use are obviously going to be limited by your diet, and some may have to come from specialist or mail-order suppliers. However, in general terms try to buy as good quality food as you can.

There is a strong argument being made by both medical practitioners and environmentalists that one of the reasons why we are seeing such a rise in food allergies and degenerative diseases is the enormous cocktail of chemicals (pesticides, fertilizers, post-harvest treatments, etc.) with which our food is drenched.

The one way that you can avoid this situation is by buying and cooking your own organically grown food (free of all chemical fertilizers, pesticides, herbicides and post-harvest treatments, or hormones and antibiotics in meat). Organic food is now a lot easier to find than it once was and, although it is still more expensive than conventionally grown or raised products, it may be worth the money if it really helps you get better.

EATING OUT
One of the hardest things for those on exclusion diets to come to terms with, is eating out—either in restaurants or with friends. Either they become paranoid (often with reason) that what they are eating may contain something that they should not have, or they become so embarrassed by the situation that they will not go out at all. But this is a great shame and quite unnecessary.

There was a time, not that long ago, when asking a restaurant to leave something out of a dish was just regarded as weird, but things are a lot better now. Food allergy has had so much publicity over the last few years that most restaurants are aware that it does exist and do at least try to be helpful.

If you are planning a meal out, call the restaurant in advance, explain your situation and ask what they have on their menu that might be suitable for you, or that they could adapt for you. Do make clear to them that this is a serious illness and that it would be dangerous for you to eat any of your forbidden foods. However, you must be aware of the hidden ingredients and point them out; you cannot expect either a chef or restaurant manager to be an expert in wheat allergy! If the restaurant is not prepared to be helpful, go elsewhere. Or, if you have no option, take your own food and tell them what you will be doing and why.

If you decide to eat out and do not have a chance to call ahead, examine everything on the menu very carefully. Go for things which are unlikely to contain wheat: no sauces or thickened soups for example, but still ask for the exact ingredients. Explain once again that you have an illness and that it is really important that you eat the right food. As of now there is no legal requirement for a restaurant to provide accurate details of ingredients to their customers, but hopefully that will soon change.

If you are traveling, and likely to have to eat out a lot, carry your own emergency rations with you: packets of gluten-free cookies, sweet and savory, are a great standby. Obviously, the longer you are traveling, the more you will need to take, but you will soon discover what you need to survive—and what you are likely to be unable to get on the road!

If eating with friends be sure to give them plenty of warning of what you can and cannot have. Your friends may be quite happy to cook something that you, along with everyone else, can eat, but if they sound at all dubious, suggest that you take along your own food. That way you will feel relaxed because you know you will not be eating anything that you shouldn't, and your host will feel equally relaxed because he or she will know that they are not feeding you anything that will make you ill.

BABIES, CHILDREN AND TEENAGERS

Having a celiac baby can be quite unnerving as you may well be a new and inexperienced parent. However, if your baby shows any of the classic symptoms (failure to thrive and gain weight, smelly stools, diarrhea, vomiting or bloating, general unwellness) go immediately to your pediatrician. Because celiac disease is fairly well recognized your doctor will no doubt pick up on it immediately. As soon as your baby is diagnosed and gluten removed from his or her diet, matters should start to improve. Do not, however, be tempted to overfeed to make up for lost time. Babies can catch up in lost growth very easily.

If your child is celiac, or has a wheat allergy and it persists, you will then find yourself with a toddler on a special diet. You obviously want to ensure that your child will not eat foods that will make him or her ill, but neither do you want to turn them into an "oddity." This should be reasonably easy at home as you should be able to convert the whole family to a mainly gluten-free diet, although this may be a little more difficult if there are older children who are free of dietary problems. However, as far as possible, make sure that all the foods that you have at home are wheat- and gluten-free, and if your child brings home friends from school, serve the friends with the same food you are all eating. They may not even notice the difference.

However, with small children you must make sure that all their relatives, their friends' parents and their school personnel are aware of their condition. Your child must also be aware of the fact that when away from home he or she must be careful and that eating things on the forbidden list will just make them feel horrible.

Make sure that they never go out without a stock of their favorite wheat- or gluten-free snacks, cookies or drinks so that when others are eating, they can too. You will also need to arrange with the school either for them to provide a gluten- or wheat-free meal or, if that is going to be difficult, for your child to take a pack lunch along.

As your toddler grows into his or her teens you may find that they are inclined to lapse from their diets. This could be because teenage is a time when many kids wish to establish their independence, and refusing to stick to the diet their parents have suggested may be one way. Other teenagers are acutely embarrassed by being seen to be "different" from their friends. Some may become lazy and not wish to bother with cooking or finding special food. Others may not react too badly to a bit of gluten or wheat in their diet and therefore assume that they need no longer bother with their diet.

Celiac disease does not go away so your teenager will probably always remain sensitive to gluten. However, it is true that they may not react too badly, or too immediately, to eating a certain amount. Although no one really knows the long-term effects of a celiac eating gluten, the chances are that a moderate amount will not do too much harm. It is therefore probably better not to have a major fight on the subject but to remain supportive so that if they do make themselves ill, you are around to help repair the damage.

Whether these comments apply also to wheat-intolerant children and teenagers will depend entirely on how sensitive they are or were to wheat and to what extent their intolerance has abated.

PREGNANCY AND CHILDBEARING

Whatever they may do in their teenage years, both boys and girls wishing to have a family will need to watch their diet. Untreated celiac disease can cause infertility in men. As far as women are concerned, it may make it more difficult for them to become pregnant, easier for them to miscarry and may cause an acute form of anemia during their pregnancy.

Although there is a slight likelihood of celiac disease or wheat sensitivity being passed from parent to child it is quite a small risk.

A FEW WARNING WORDS

- Always eat before you go out to a party so that if there is nothing there that you can eat you will not be racked with pangs of hunger all night.
- Always carry a snack with you when you go out in case your plans change and you cannot find anything that you are allowed to eat. You can always drink water if there is nothing else, but if there are only sandwiches to eat you are stuck!
- Never accept someone's word that the food they are offering you is wheat- or gluten-free unless you are really sure they know what they are saying; people often assure you that things are safe when they really do not know and are just trying to be helpful.
- If you have to go into a hospital, check with the hospital as to their provision of wheat- or gluten-free food—there is no guarantee that they will be able to provide it. You may either need to get a family member or friend to cook your own food and bring it in or prepare lots for yourself before-hand and bring it in with you.
- Do not be tempted, just because you are feeling so much better, to assume that you are cured! Celiacs are rarely cured at all and even wheat intolerants may have to spend a couple of years avoiding wheat before their system will tolerate it again. Be warned that if your body has just started to recover it will be even more sensitive to the food it didn't tolerate and its reaction will be dramatic.

PRESCRIPTIONS

Registered celiacs can get certain special foods on prescription. However, now that prescription charges have risen so much, it may be cheaper to buy the special diet food than to pay the prescription charge. However, it is worth checking this out with your doctor or pharmacist.

THE RECIPES

The recipes that follow are, naturally, all wheat- and gluten-free. However, they are not all for dishes in which you would normally expect to find either wheat or gluten. Since it is recognized that over-indulgence is one of the causes of food intolerance one of the first things that wheat intolerants or celiac should do is try to broaden their diet. And it is amazing, once you start to look around, how many dishes there are that do not, and never have, contained either wheat or gluten.

There are, of course, many recipes for foods which you would naturally expect to be made of wheat flour: cakes, cookies, pastries, pastas, sauces, thickened soups, etc. Although there are a number of wheat- and/or gluten-free "mixes" on the market, we have chosen (with the exception of pasta) to use natural ingredients rather than packet mixes. This is partially because we feel that if you are to start a new regime cooking yourself real food; you should cook with real food and partly because the mixes tend to be a great deal more expensive than the raw materials.

With regard to pasta, you can make your own and indeed may need to do so if you live away from a main shopping center; it will also be a lot cheaper than buying it ready made. However, it is a good deal more bother so we normally suggest using one of the many proprietary brands available either in health food stores or via mail order.

My "raw materials" have been garbanzo (chick pea) flour (used widely in Indian cooking), rice flour, corn flour or cornmeal, oatmeal, potato flour, cornstarch, soy flour and buckwheat flour. All of these should be available at health food sections in your supermarket or at health food stores. Garbanzo flour is sometimes combined with fava bean flour (garbanzo/fava bean flour), and this product will work admirably in recipes calling for garbanzo flour. Check the packages to make sure that none of these are milled with wheat flour; if they are the risk of contamination may be quite great.

Of all the baked goods, cakes, when excluding wheat flour, work the best, and I would defy anyone to tell that many of the cakes in the cake section were not made with wheat flour.

Pastry and cookies work pretty well although the lack of gluten prevents them from holding together as well as a wheat-based mixture. However, as long as you are prepared to put up with them being a bit crumbly, the flavor is very good.

My personal taste, in a number of recipes that require a "heavier" sweetener, is for raw cane, or "turbinado," sugar, which contains the molasses part of the sugar. In these particular recipes, the words "raw cane" appear in parentheses after "sugar." Raw cane (turbinado-style) sugar may be substituted on a one-for-one basis with regular granulated sugar.

Potato flour and cornstarch make very successful thickeners for sauces, soups or anything else.

The only area that presents real problems is bread, especially as we are used to the risen, soft breads which depend heavily on a high gluten content. There are recipes for half a dozen delicious and well-textured breads in the baking section of the book (thanks to the ingenuity and skills of my good friend and colleague Miriam Polunin) but they are not, and never will be, Mother's Pride!

Dishes that do not, and never did, use wheat flour speak for themselves.

A final note: You will see the abbreviation hpg used in some of the recipes; this means heaping. All other spoonfuls are level.

Happy Cooking!

Once again, make sure to read packages and labels to make sure that offending wheat and/or gluten products are not included in the ingredients you buy. The recipes in this book have been carefully checked and tested, but we cannot be responsible for inadvertent contamination occurring in stores or homes or for adverse reactions resulting from consumption of any of the foods listed in the recipes.

Soups, Starters and Light Lunches

Sweet Potato Soup with
Coriander and Ginger

Cream of Mushroom Soup

Creamed Green Pea Soup
with Pine Nuts

Kidney Soup

Leek, Potato and Smoked Mackerel Soup

Bacon, Apple and Sausage Pie

Smoked Fish Pâté

"Seedy" Pastry Squares

Sweet Pepper Pâté

Terrine of Chicken and Walnuts

Polenta with Gorgonzola

Steamed Potatoes with Walnut Sauce

Eggs Florentine

Cheese Sables

Herb and Bacon Pie

Crudités and Dips

French Toast with Bacon

Vol au Vent Shells

Not only are sweet potatoes delicious to eat but they are an excellent source of Vitamin E, potassium and iron. The orange variety is also high in the anti-oxidant vitamins thought to be protective against cancer.

Sweet Potato Soup with Coriander and Ginger

Serves 6

This is the most wonderfully warm soup for a cold evening—yet it works equally well chilled on a hot summer night !

1 lb 5oz	sweet potatoes
7oz	ordinary potatoes
1 inch	cube of fresh gingerroot, peeled
4	large cloves of garlic
1¾ pints	water
3½ fl oz	medium sherry
	salt
	pepper
	large bunch of fresh coriander

Peel the sweet potatoes and scrub the ordinary potatoes. Cut them into large dice and put them in a deep pot with the fresh gingerroot, the garlic cloves, peeled but whole, and the water. Bring to a boil and simmer for 30–40 minutes or until the vegetables are thoroughly cooked. Purée in a food processor then return to the pot, add the sherry and season to taste with salt and pepper. Just before serving add the chopped coriander.

PER SERVING	
Calories	137.33
Protein g	2.32
Fat g	.42
Saturated fatty acids g	.45
Monounsaturated fatty acids g	1.38
Polyunsaturated fatty acids g	.15
Carbohydrate g	28.61
Total Sugars g	6.67
Sodium mg	173.49
Fiber g	3.00

If you want a puréed rather than a chunky soup, put the mixture through a food processor, then sieve it before returning it to the pan, adding the cream and adjusting the seasoning.

Cream of Mushroom Soup

Serves 6

A classic mushroom soup which is given a lovely fresh flavor by the lemon juice.

1/2	Spanish onion, very thinly sliced
2 tbsp	olive oil
8 oz	button mushrooms, thinly sliced
	juice 1 lemon
1 tbsp	cornstarch
1 pint	chicken stock
1/2 pint	milk
5 fl oz	dry white wine
	salt
	pepper
4 fl oz	fresh heavy cream

Heat the oil in a heavy pan and gently cook the onion until it is transparent and softening but not colored. When the onion is soft, add the mushrooms and lemon juice and cook them altogether for a couple of minutes; do not let them brown. Add the cornstarch, stir for a minute or two, then gradually add the stock, milk and white wine. Bring the mixture to a boil and simmer gently for 15 minutes. Season to taste with salt and freshly ground pepper (white if possible). Just before serving add the cream and adjust the seasoning.

PER SERVING	
Calories	423.91
Protein g	18.11
Fat g	30.61
Saturated fatty acids g	7.01
MonounSaturated fatty acids g	6.80
PolyunSaturated fatty acids g	1.02
Carbohydrate g	16.33
Total Sugars g	5.28
Sodium mg	164.68
Fiber g	.44

Although fresh young green peas in summer are a real treat, frozen peas are picked and frozen straight from the plant so are often even fresher than those you shell yourself. The frozen variety also retains all the high levels of vitamins and minerals to be found in the fresh.

Creamed Green Pea Soup with Pine Nuts

Serves 4

This recipe is based on a sixteenth-century Italian dish and is both unusual and delicious. It is also very substantial so could be used as a main course for lunch or a light dinner.

18 oz	frozen green peas
4	trimmed green onions, chopped roughly
1	can of sweetcorn (14 oz), drained
1 pint	chicken stock or water
3–4 tbsp	medium sherry (optional)
	sea salt
	freshly ground black pepper
2 tbsp	pine nuts
2 tbsp	freshly grated Parmesan

Put the peas, with the green onions and corn, in a deep pan and add the stock. Bring to a boil and simmer for 20 minutes. Purée in a food processor or liquidizer. If you want a smooth purée you will also need to put the soup through a sieve to remove the remaining husk. Return the soup to the pan, add the sherry and season to taste with sea salt and freshly ground black pepper.

Meanwhile, pulverize the pine nuts in a processor but be careful to be brief as you want them to remain fairly coarse. Mix them with the Parmesan.

To serve, reheat the soup, put it into bowls and sprinkle each liberally with the pine nut and Parmesan mixture.

PER SERVING	
Calories	683.25
Protein g	41.24
Fat g	40.04
Saturated fatty acids g	3.55
Polyunsaturated fatty acids g	6.35
Monounsaturated fatty acids g	4.11
Carbohydrate g	38.96
Total Sugars g	9.06
Englyst fiber g	7.90
Sodium mg	631.22

Although organ meats are no longer very popular, they are very nutritious. Kidneys especially are rich in protein, niacin, iron, zinc, copper, selenium and the A and B vitamins. If your family does not like the texture of kidney, cook all the kidneys with the garlic and onion and purée everything together. The kidney texture will not be so noticeable.

Kidney Soup

Serves 6

A good old fashioned soup for a cold winter's evening.

3 tbsp	olive oil
8 oz	onions, sliced thinly
2	cloves garlic, chopped finely
1	small carrot, diced
12 oz	lambs' kidneys, trimmed and diced
4 oz	mushrooms, diced
2 tbsp	fresh parsley, chopped
2	bay leaves
5 fl oz	port (optional)
2 pints	water
2 tsp	anchovy paste (Check that it is gluten free)
1 tsp	black peppercorns
	salt
	pepper

Heat half the oil in a deep, heavy pan and fry the onion, garlic and carrot briskly until they are lightly tanned and just softening. Then add 8 oz of the kidneys and all the mushrooms and continue to cook, more gently, for a couple of minutes or until the kidneys no longer look pink.

Add the parsley, bay leaves, port, water, anchovy paste and peppercorns, bring to a boil, cover and simmer gently for 45 minutes. Purée the soup in a processor. Meanwhile, lightly fry the remaining kidney pieces in the rest of the oil. Return the soup to the pan, add the kidney and juice, reheat gently and season to taste with salt and a little more pepper if needed.

PER SERVING	
Calories	185.24
Protein g	11.01
Fat g	9.39
Saturated fatty acids g	2.01
MonounSaturated fatty acids g	6.26
PolyunSaturated fatty acids g	1.22
Carbohydrate g	7.85
Total Sugars g	6.13
Sodium mg	282.3
Fiber g	1.27

If you have leftover smoked mackerel, it makes excellent sandwiches either in wheat/gluten-free bread or between pancakes. Just add a squeeze of lemon juice.

Leek, Potato and Smoked Mackerel Soup

Serves 4

"There's eating and drinking," as the saying goes, in this soup. Serve as a main meal with a salad or some cheese to follow.

5 oz	leeks, washed, trimmed and sliced
10 oz	potatoes, scrubbed and diced
4 oz	peppered smoked mackerel fillets, skinned
1¾ pints	water
5 fl oz	medium sherry (optional)

Put the leeks, potatoes and ¾ of the mackerel into a large saucepan with the water. Bring to boil and simmer gently for 15–20 minutes or until the potatoes are quite cooked. Remove from the pan and purée in a food processor. Return to the saucepan and add the rest of the smoked mackerel, broken into small pieces, and the sherry if you are using it.

You should not need any further seasoning of any kind, but taste to make sure. The soup is delicious just as it is but if you want, you can add chopped parsley or a swirl of cream to each portion just before serving.

PER SERVING	
Calories	197.25
Protein g	6.94
Fat g	8.06
Saturated fatty acids g	2.36
MonounSaturated fatty acids g	4.90
PolyunSaturated fatty acids g	1.76
Carbohydrate g	15.34
Total Sugars g	2.63
Sodium mg	195.75
Fiber g	1.80

This savory pie is excellent served warm, in little finger slices, for a cocktail or buffet party.

Bacon, Apple and Sausage Pie

Serves 6

This is an excellent dish for children or for a buffet party. It can be made in advance and frozen or just reheated. It also tastes excellent cold.

90 oz	sifted garbanzo (garbanzo/fava bean) flour
3 oz	butter or margarine
2 tbsp	water
7 oz	bacon slices, roughly chopped
1	medium onion, roughly chopped
4 oz	Wheat- and gluten-free sausage meat
1 oz	oatmeal (leave these out if you are not allowed oats)
2	eating apples, peeled
	salt
	pepper
	pinch dried thyme
1	small onion, sliced into rings
1 oz	melted butter

Heat the oven to 375°F.

Rub the butter or margarine into the flour then mix to a soft dough with 2–3 tbsps of water. Roll out and line an 8-inch pie pan with the pastry.

Fry the bacon with the chopped onion in a pan for 5 minutes or until the bacon is beginning to soften and color slightly. Work in the sausage meat and continue to cook for a further 5 minutes. Add one of the apples, chopped small, with the oats if you are using them, a little seasoning and thyme. Spoon the mixture into the middle of the pan and spread it out evenly. Slice the other apple and lay it over the sausage mixture along with the onion rings. Brush them all with the melted butter.

Bake the pie, uncovered, for 40–45 minutes. If the apple and onion look like they are burning, cover them with a piece of foil. Serve warm or cold with a salad.

PER SERVING	
Calories	433.09
Protein g	12.48
Fat g	34.39
Saturated fatty acids g	16.80
Monounsaturated fatty acids g	12.48
Polyunsaturated fatty acids g	3.21
Carbohydrate g	19.89
Total Sugars g	2.96
Sodium mg	786.30
Englyst fiber g	3.51

Smoked salmon is also good in scrambled eggs or in an omelette. You can buy several packets and freeze them for future use.

Smoked Fish Pâté

Serves 6

An excellent standby pâté. You can use smoked salmon available from most supermarkets if you want to be extravagant, or stick with the less expensive smoked mackerel.

7 oz	smoked mackerel fillet or any other smoked fish of your choice
4 oz	soft butter
4 oz	plain cream cheese
1½	slices wheat- and gluten-free brown bread
	salt
	freshly ground black pepper
	juice of 2–3 lemons

Remove the skin and any bones from the fish and flake it into a mixing bowl with the butter and cream cheese. Beat well with a wooden spoon or an electric mixer until they are amalgamated. If you want a very smooth purée, you could beat them in a food processor.

Crumb the slices of bread and beat into the pâté.

Season to taste with salt, freshly ground pepper and the lemon juice and serve with rice cakes or gluten- and wheat-free toast.

PER SERVING	
Calories	287.92
Protein g	8.61
Fat g	25.55
Saturated fatty acids g	12.08
Monounsaturated fatty acids g	8.93
Polyunsaturated fatty acids g	2.82
Carbohydrate g	7.03
Total Sugars g	1.95
Sodium mg	480.33
Fiber g	.46

These would be useful crackers to carry with you as snacks if you were going out and thought that you would not be able to find any wheat/gluten-free foods.

"Seedy" Pastry Squares

Serves 10

These are delicious little crackers that can be used as cocktail snacks with a drink, with soup or even with cheese.

7 oz	sifted garbanzo (garbanzo/fava bean) flour or rice flour or a combination of the two
4 oz	butter
	water
1	egg, beaten
1 tbsp	sesame, sunflower, poppy seeds or aniseeds
	sea salt

Rub the butter into the flour then mix to a soft dough with 2–3 tablespoons of water. Roll out to approximately ¼ inch thickness and paint with the beaten egg. Sprinkle with a little salt and the seed of your choice, cut into squares and bake for 10–15 minutes on a greased baking sheet, taking great care that they do not burn. Serve warm.

PER SERVING	
Calories	160.07
Protein g	5.20
Fat g	11.35
Saturated fatty acids g	5.89
Monounsaturated fatty acids g	3.02
Polyunsaturated fatty acids g	1.51
Carbohydrate g	10.10
Total Sugars g	.69
Sodium mg	208.25
Fiber g	2.34

Like any other soft pâté, *Ajwar* can also be used as a dip with fresh vegetable crudités or with a salad.

Sweet Pepper Pâté

Serves 6

Known as *Ajwar* in southeast Europe (the dish comes from the former Yugoslavia), this pâté uses the sweet red bell peppers so beloved of the Hungarians to make a spectacularly colored and very tasty pâté.

2	medium eggplant, thickly sliced
3 tbsp	olive oil
2	large red bell peppers, deseeded and chopped
3	large cloves of garlic
	salt
	pepper

In a wide pan, fry the eggplant slices in the oil until they are nicely browned on each side. Put all the ingredients except the salt and pepper in a food processor and purée. The pâté should not be totally smooth when processed but have the texture of a country terrine. Season to taste and serve chilled with crackers or toast.

PER SERVING	
Calories	111.21
Protein g	2.18
Fat g	8.32
Saturated fatty acids g	1.25
Monounsaturated fatty acids g	7.25
Polyunsaturated fatty acids g	1.25
Carbohydrate g	7.61
Total Sugars g	6.77
Sodium mg	70.41
Fiber g	3.84

This terrine is great for a buffet party as it can be eaten with a fork and looks really pretty when laid out on a serving dish with some watercress.

Terrine of Chicken and Walnuts

Serves 6

An old favorite, this terrine keeps well and slices excellently for a lunch or buffet party. The walnuts turn a light purple color as they cook and make the terrine look a lot more interesting!

1	small chicken
1 pint	water
9 oz	unsmoked slab of fresh bacon
2 oz	broken walnuts
	salt
10	peppercorns, lightly crushed
1	small clove garlic, crushed
1 tbsp	brandy (optional)

Poach the chicken in the water for 30–40 minutes or until it is cooked. Remove the chicken, cool it slightly, then remove the flesh and chop it into reasonably small pieces. Reduce the stock by boiling it fast for about 10 minutes.

Boil the bacon in unsalted water for about 20 minutes or until it is cooked. Cool, then dice it. Mix the chicken in a bowl with the bacon, walnuts, salt, peppercorns, garlic and brandy. Add 1/3 cup of the reduced stock and mix it in well.

Heat the oven to 350°F.

Grease a round, oval or rectangular terrine dish and spoon the mixture in. Cover and bake, in a bain marie,* for 75 minutes. Remove the terrine from the oven, cool it slightly, then remove the cover and replace it with a weighted board; refrigerate for at least 12 hours.

When it is absolutely cold, turn it out and slice it to serve. Serve as a starter with crackers or toast or as a light lunch dish with a salad.

PER SERVING	
Calories	442.45
Protein g	41.53
Fat g	29.95
Saturated fatty acids g	9.43
Monounsaturated fatty acids g	11.67
Polyunsaturated fatty acids g	7.17
Carbohydrate g	.44
Total Sugars g	.26
Sodium mg	942.76
Fiber g	.33

* A baking pan containing water, which will "soften" the cooking. Be sure not to let the water boil for fear of condensation getting into the cooking dish.

The polenta is also excellent served warm, buttered and covered with paper-thin slivers of Parmesan

Polenta with Gorgonzola

Serves 4

Polenta is currently all the rage in smart restaurants—which is great for people who cannot eat wheat or gluten. For once a "special diet" is actually fashionable! Cook the polenta in a non-stick saucepan, if you have one; otherwise it will glue itself to the pan.

4 oz	coarse polenta
18 fl oz	water
4 oz	Gorgonzola
	sea salt

Heat the oven to 350°F.

Bring the water to a simmer with the salt. Gradually add the polenta to the water (Italians let it run through their fingers) stirring all the time. Bring back to a simmer and cook, stirring all the time, for 5 minutes. Oil a shallow ovenproof dish and spoon in the polenta mix; it should be about 1 inch deep. Cover with oiled foil and bake for 1 hour.

Take out of the oven and, with the foil still on top, allow it to get quite cold.

When ready to serve, heat the broiler. Turn the polenta out onto a board and slice in ½-inch squares, or cut into triangles. Broil the slices on one side until they are tanned and crisp. Turn the slices and broil lightly on second side. Slice the Gorgonzola and lay it over the polenta. Continue to broil until the cheese is melted and lightly browned.

Serve at once.

PER SERVING	
Calories	182.00
Protein g	7.25
Fat g	9.18
Saturated fatty acids g	5.18
MonounSaturated fatty acids g	2.00
PolyunSaturated fatty acids g	.38
Carbohydrate g	18.13
Total Sugars g	.25
Sodium mg	612.00
Fiber g	0

Few people think of eating potatoes by themselves although they are really delicious, especially the little early season ones. Try them steamed until just soft and served with melted butter or a good olive oil and freshly grated sea salt.

Steamed Potatoes with Walnut Sauce

Serves 4

This dish hails from South America where the potato is valued as a food in its own right—not just as an accompaniment to other things. Serve it as a light lunch or supper dish as it is rather too substantial for a starter—unless you have a very hungry family !

14 oz	new potatoes
4 tbsp	walnut or sunflower oil
1	small onion, sliced thickly
2	cloves garlic, finely chopped
3	small green chilies, deseeded and finely chopped (if using dried chilies you will need to soak them in boiling water first)
2 oz	broken walnuts
2 oz	crumbly white cheese (such as Lancashire or shredded white cheddar)
7 oz	cooked shrimps or prawns
9 fl oz	milk
	salt

Steam or microwave the potatoes until cooked, then halve them lengthways. Meanwhile, heat the oil and gently fry the onion and garlic over a low heat until the onion is golden. Put the oil, onions, garlic, chilies, walnuts, cheese and half the shrimps or prawns in a food processor and purée, gradually adding the milk to reduce the consistency to a thick sauce. Add extra milk or oil if it seems too thick. Season to taste with salt.

While the potatoes are still warm, lay them out on a serving dish, pour over the sauce and decorate with the remaining shrimps or prawns.

The dish is best eaten when the potatoes are just warm but if you want to prepare it ahead of time and eat it cold it is still excellent.

PER SERVING	
Calories	417.9
Protein g	18.47
Fat g	29.27
Saturated fatty acids g	5.58
Monounsaturated fatty acids g	6.83
Polyunsaturated fatty acids g	16.74
Carbohydrate g	21.68
Total Sugars g	6.00
Sodium mg	708.01
Fiber g	1.8

Important note
Do bear in mind that egg yolks should be cooked hard for total safety especially if they are to be eaten by children, pregnant mothers or elderly people.

Eggs Florentine

Serves 4

This is a more substantial variation on classic Eggs Florentine. However you need to keep a close eye on the eggs while they cook, as depending on the accuracy of your oven and the size of the eggs, they may take more or less than the 15 minutes given.

3 tbsp	olive oil
9 oz	mushrooms, sliced
1 lb 2 oz	fresh spinach, well washed and dried
1 tbsp	pumpkin seeds
4	large eggs
2 tbsp	Cheddar cheese, grated
2 tbsp	Swiss cheese, grated
5 tbsp	plain low-fat yogurt
	salt
	freshly ground black pepper

Heat the oven to 325°F.

Heat the oil in a large pan and briskly cook the mushrooms for a couple of minutes. Add the spinach and let it wilt briefly, then mix in the pumpkin seeds and season lightly. Spoon the spinach into an ovenproof dish and make hollows for the eggs. Break in the eggs. Mix the cheeses and the yogurt together and spoon it over the eggs.

Bake for 15 minutes in a moderate oven (or 5 minutes in a microwave on High) or until the eggs are just set. Serve at once.

PER SERVING	
Calories	352.03
Protein g	19.55
Fat g	28.5
Saturated fatty acids g	8.22
MonounSaturated fatty acids g	13.91
PolyunSaturated fatty acids g	4.39
Carbohydrate g	5.23
Total Sugars g	4.09
Sodium mg	501.9
Fiber g	3.64

As an alternative cocktail snack, do not roll the mixture flat but into little balls in your hands; then roll them in the sesame seeds. They will need to cook for a little longer as they will be thicker.

Cheese Sables

Serves 10, 2 per serving

Delicious cheesey biscuits which can be used as a cocktail snack or with cheese. The quantities in this recipe will make approximately 20 cocktail-sized biscuits.

4 oz	garbanzo (garbanzo/fava bean) flour
1 oz	butter
2 tbsp	sharp Cheddar cheese, grated
1–2 tbsp	water
1	egg yolk
2 tbsp	sesame seeds (optional)

Sieve the flour and cut in the butter. Rub in the butter with the cheese. Mix to a soft dough with the water then roll out on a well-floured board. It will stick slightly but if you roll with care and keep a spatula and some extra flour available it should be fine. Roll to a thickness of about ½ inch, then cut out with a small round cutter. Brush the top of each biscuit generously with the egg yolk and sprinkle with the sesame seeds. Place on an oiled baking sheet.

Bake in a moderate oven (350°F) for 10–15 minutes until the biscuits are lightly tanned and crisp but take care that they do not burn. Cool on a rack before serving.

PER SERVING	
Calories	167.65
Protein g	6.76
Fat g	12.16
Saturated fatty acids g	5.07
Monounsaturated fatty acids g	3.69
Polyunsaturated fatty acids g	2.49
Carbohydrate g	8.42
Total Sugars g	.55
Sodium mg	91.67
Fiber g	2.31

Herb and Bacon Pie

Serves 6

This is based on a recipe for a medieval pie which accounts for the large variety of herbs, as in the Middle Ages they were virtually interchangeable with vegetables.

3 oz	rice flour, brown if possible
3 oz	garbanzo (garbanzo/fava bean) flour
3 oz	butter or margarine
12 oz	bacon slices
8 oz	leeks, cleaned and sliced thickly
8 oz	fresh spinach, cleaned and roughly chopped
1	bunches watercress, stalks removed
1	handful fresh parsley
2	sprigs fresh thyme, stalks removed or 1/2 teaspoon dried
2	fresh sage leaves or 1/2 teaspoon dried
3	medium eggs
5 fl oz	chicken stock or water
	black pepper

Heat the oven to 350°F.

Mix the flours together then rub in the butter until the mixture is the texture of breadcrumbs. Add enough cold water to make a firm dough and set aside.

Remove the rinds from the bacon and grill the slices until crisp. Line an 8-inch pie pan with half the bacon. Mix the leeks, spinach, watercress and herbs and pile them on top of the bacon. Beat the eggs together, set aside a little egg with which to brush the top of the pie, then add the stock to the rest. Season with freshly ground black pepper (the bacon should be salty enough not to need any extra) and pour over the vegetables. Lay the remaining bacon over the vegetables.

On a well-floured (rice or garbanzo) board, roll out the pastry quite thickly. Place the pie dish on the pastry and cut out its shape. Use the trimmings to line the edge of the dish. Carefully lift the pastry on a rolling pin and cover the pie. Use the trimmings to decorate its top and brush with the reserved beaten egg.

PER SERVING	
Calories	552.74
Protein g	21.5
Fat g	42.67
Saturated fatty acids g	14.92
Polyunsaturated fatty acids g	4.83
Monounsaturated fatty acids g	16.78
Carbohydrate g	21.28
Total Sugars g	2.88
Fiber g	3.79
Sodium mg	5141.08

Bake the pie for 30–40 minutes or until the pastry is crisp and golden. Serve warm rather than hot.

Crudités and Dips

Crudités are ideal for anyone with a gluten or wheat intolerance as the vegetables are all perfectly safe and it is easy to make dips that will also be wheat- and gluten-free. If you want to vary the textures, you can include potato or tortilla chips.

You will need up to 9 oz of vegetables per person and around 3½ oz of dip.

Ingredients:
Any raw vegetable, with the possible exception of potatoes, is good for crudités. Try to use contrasting colors and shapes on a serving platter or restrict the vegetables to one or two colors for effect. Use:

Artichokes (Jerusalem) or globe leaves; **beans**—green, French, etc.—raw or lightly cooked; **beets**—raw or lightly cooked; **broccoli florets**—raw or lightly cooked; **Brussels sprouts**—raw or lightly cooked; **cabbage**—green, red, Chinese leaves, etc.—raw; **carrots**—raw; **cauliflower florets**—raw or lightly cooked; **celery**—raw; **chicory**—raw; **zucchini**—raw; **baby corns**—raw; **cucumber**; **fennel**—raw or lightly cooked; **snow peas**—raw; **mushrooms**—raw; **parsnips**—raw; **peppers**—red, green, yellow, black—raw; **radishes**; **spring onions**; **baby tomatoes**; **turnips** or anything else that appeals.

Dips
Ready-made: taramasalata, hummus, tahini, raita—but check ingredients for wheat or gluten.
Homemade: Choose among ingredients: start with mayonnaise (bought or homemade but not salad dressing), yogurt, heavy cream, light cream or cottage cheese.
Add: horseradish sauce, curry paste (check ingredients) and a little apricot jam, mustard of any kind (check ingredients), tomato purée or lots of chopped fresh herbs.
Season with: salt and pepper, lemon juice, tabasco (a little), and any chopped herb but try to avoid using dried herbs or spices as they tend to taste raw when they are not cooked.

It is not possible to give a nutritional analysis as the ingredients could be so different.

French toast is excellent just with bacon but you can make it into a more substantial dish by serving it with wheat/gluten-free sausages or with jam or fruit jelly.

French Toast with Bacon

Serves 6

French toast is normally one of those delicious dishes banned to those on a wheat- or gluten-free diet although it actually works very well with both homemade and purchased wheat/gluten-free breads.

6	eggs
6 fl oz	milk
½ tsp	ground cinnamon
2 oz	poppy seeds
	salt and pepper
6	large thick slices of wheat- and gluten-free bread
12 oz	lean bacon slices
1 oz	butter

Whisk the eggs with the milk, cinnamon and poppy seeds in a large, flat dish. Season with pepper only. Submerge the slices of bread in the mixture and, if you have time, leave them to soak for half an hour.

To cook, fry the bacon in its own fat until it is tanned but not burned. Remove with a slotted spoon, drain on a piece of paper towel and keep warm. Tip the bacon fat into a large, clean frying pan with the butter and heat gently. With a spatula, transfer the bread slices to the pan and fry them gently on both sides until they are lightly browned and slightly puffed. Serve them at once with the bacon.

PER SERVING	
Calories	542.46
Protein g	22.4
Fat g	40.55
Saturated fatty acids g	14.8
MonounSaturated fatty acids g	16.46
PolyunSaturated fatty acids g	5.61
Carbohydrate g	24.21
Total Sugars g	3.87
Sodium mg	1293.37
Fiber g	2.41

Puff and flaky pastry are difficult for any cook to make so if you succeed with a wheat/gluten-free pastry, you can count yourself a real pastry chef !

Vol au Vent Shells

Serves 8

These vol au vent shells can be filled with any filling of your choice and served either hot or cold.

5 oz	sifted garbanzo (garbanzo/fava bean) flour
	pinch of salt
4 oz	butter
	water

Sift the flour into a bowl with the salt. Cut the butter into walnut-size pieces and mix it into the flour in lumps. Add approximately 4 tablespoons of chilled water to make a firm dough. Put it to chill in a plastic bag in the fridge for 15 minutes.

On a floured board, lay out the pastry. Working as for puff pastry (bring the rolling pin down quite heavily on the pastry and then give it a quick roll backwards and forward; do not push as with ordinary pastry or the butter will be moved out of place), roll to a strip about 6 inches long and 2 inches thick. Fold in three, turn the pastry so that the open edge is facing you and roll again, this time to around 1 1/2 inch in thickness. Fold in three and set aside to cool again for 15 minutes. Repeat this process twice more.

To make the shells heat the oven to 350°F.

Roll the pastry out again (this amount of pastry will make 8 medium-sized vol au vents or 12 cocktail size) to around 1 1/2 inch thickness. Use a pastry cutter or a glass to cut out 8 rounds. Then use a small cutter or glass to make a small circle inside each round, but take care not to go through the pastry.

Place on a greased baking sheet and cook for 10–15 minutes until the pastry is slightly risen, tanned and crisp.

Remove carefully to a rack and, with a sharp knife, remove each "lid" from the center of each vol au vent and set aside. Remove any uncooked dough from the inside of the shell. Fill with the filling of your choice and replace the lid to serve.

PER SERVING	
Calories	173.84
Protein g	3.77
Fat g	13.78
Saturated fatty acids g	8.53
MonounSaturated fatty acids g	3.3
PolyunSaturated fatty acids g	.91
Carbohydrate g	9.46
Total Sugars g	.64
Sodium mg	148.78
Fiber g	2.01

Fish

Salmon en Croûte

Kedgeree

Persian Squid Pilaff

Tuna Curry with Coconut and Cilantro

Salmon, Apple and Peanut Salad

Salmon en Papillotte

Edward Abbott's Shellfish Salad

Dutch Herring and Beet Salad

Fish Crumble

Guyanan Okra with Shrimp

Crab Cobbler

Ever Popular Fish Cakes

Paella

Stir-Fried Artichokes with Tuna

Salmon en Croûte

Serves 6

This classic Russian recipe, often called Salmon Koulibiac, makes a great dish for a dinner party or a buffet. It looks impressive, is pretty filling, but not expensive to make.

10 oz	fresh salmon, fillet or cutlets
2	slices of lemon
7 oz	brown rice
7 oz	sifted garbanzo (garbanzo/fava bean) flour
4 oz	butter
1 tbsp	olive oil
1	medium onion, finely chopped
2 oz	mushrooms, finely chopped
	large handful of fresh parsley, chopped
	juice of 2 lemons
2	eggs
small tsp	salt
	black pepper

Heat the oven to 350°F.

Put the salmon in a large, shallow pan with the lemon slices. Cover with water, bring slowly to a boil and simmer for 8–10 minutes or until it is cooked through.

Remove the fish and set it aside, discard the lemon slices and add the rice to the water. Bring back to a boil and boil briskly for 15 minutes or until the rice is cooked. Add more water if it looks as though it is drying out.

Rub the butter into the flour and mix to a soft dough with a couple of tablespoons of water. Take ⅓ of the dough and roll it out into a circle slightly less than ½ inch thick and place it on a greased baking pan. Do not worry if the pastry crumbles somewhat; just stick it back together with a little water. Bake this pastry "plate" in the oven for 15 minutes or until it is crisp.

Meanwhile, heat the oil in a heavy pan and add the onion and mushrooms. Cook together gently for 5–8 minutes or until they are cooked through.

When the rice is cooked, drain it, put it into a bowl and add the onion and mushroom mixture. Flake in the salmon and then add

PER SERVING	
Calories	499.58
Protein g	21.21
Fat g	27.36
Saturated fatty acids g	11.85
Monounsaturated fatty acids g	9.62
Polyunsaturated fatty acids g	4.13
Carbohydrate g	45.89
Total Sugars g	3.14
Sodium mg	542.58
Fiber g	4.75

the parsley, lemon juice, salt and pepper. Beat the eggs in a bowl and add most of them, reserving a little to paint the top crust. Mix it all together thoroughly.

Pile the rice and fish mixture on top of the cooked pastry. Roll out the remaining pastry and cover the rice mixture with it, pressing down the edges to make a seal. Once again, do not worry if it falls apart. Just patch it and paint generously with the reserved egg. You can also use the pastry trimmings to decorate the top crust.

Return to the oven for another 20 minutes or until the pastry is cooked and lightly browned.

Serve hot with a moist vegetable, such as a ratatouille, or cold (at room temperature) with a salad.

Kedgeree appeared on every grand Edwardian breakfast table along with the kidneys and bacon and the cold roasts from the night before. It then graduated to a brunch dish and has now come full circle and is served in smart restaurants as a lunch or supper dish.

Kedgeree

Serves 6

The classic fish dish from Britain's Indian empire. Being rice based it is fine for those on wheat- or gluten-free diets, but check that the curry powder you have does not contain wheat starch.

12 oz	smoked haddock fillets
6 oz	long-grain rice
1	small onion
1 oz	butter
3 oz	raisins
2 tsp	wheat- and gluten-free curry powder
3 tbsp	olive oil
1	hard boiled egg
	juice of 1 lemon

Put the fish on to poach for 10 minutes in gently boiling water. At the same time cook the rice in boiling water for approximately 10 minutes or until it is just cooked. Chop the onion finely and fry it gently in the butter until it is soft but not colored.

While the onion and rice are cooking, pour boiling water over the raisins and soak them for 10 minutes.

Drain and flake the fish; drain and rinse the rice in boiling water and drain the raisins. Set all aside to be amalgamated into the final dish.

Use either a double boiler or an ovenproof dish with a lid. Put the fried onion in the bottom and cover it with the raisins and then with the flaked fish. Heat the oil and mix it with the curry powder to make a paste. Mix this into the rice and spoon the rice over the fish.

Cover the dish with a tea cloth and then with the lid so that it is well sealed. If in a double boiler, simmer for 25 minutes; if in a casserole, cook in a slow oven (300°F) for 25 minutes.

To serve, heat a flat dish and turn the kedgeree out onto it so that the fish, raisins, etc., are uppermost. Finely chop the hard boiled egg, sprinkle it over the top and pour over the lemon juice. Serve at once.

PER SERVING	
Calories	307.37
Protein g	15.11
Fat g	12.67
Saturated fatty acids g	3.89
Monounsaturated fatty acids g	6.81
Polyunsaturated fatty acids g	1.30
Carbohydrate g	33.94
Total Sugars g	9.96
Sodium mg	497.38
Fiber g	.47

Anyone who feels squeamish about squid (and many people do) may substitute shrimps for the squid in this recipe and it will taste just as good.

Persian Squid Pilaff

Serves 6

If you can get the ink from the squid you can turn this into an even more exotic dish by adding the ink to the cooking liquid—and turning the whole dish black !

5 tbsp	olive oil
1	medium onion, peeled and chopped finely
2	large yellow bell peppers
2	cloves garlic, finely chopped
9 oz	long-grain white rice
1 tsp	ground allspice
1 tsp	ground cumin
2 tsp	dried mint
7 oz	prepared squid, fresh or frozen, sliced
2 oz	currants
	salt
	pepper
	juice 2 large lemons
	large handful of fresh coriander, chopped

Heat the oil in a large, shallow pan and gently cook the onion, peppers and garlic until they are soft but not browned. Add the rice, spices and herbs and stir for a few minutes, then add enough water to cover the rice. Bring the mixture to a boil and simmer, with the pan uncovered, for 10–15 minutes or until the rice is just cooked but not mushy. (You may have to add a little extra water if it dries up too fast.) Add the squid, currants and seasoning to taste. Cook for a few more minutes, then add the lemon juice and coriander. Serve warm or cold with a green salad.

PER SERVING	
Calories	333.00
Protein g	9.15
Fat g	13.63
Saturated fatty acids g	2.70
Monounsaturated fatty acids g	9.70
Polyunsaturated fatty acids g	1.62
Carbohydrate g	44.29
Total Sugars g	10.65
Sodium mg	133.14
Fiber g	1.60

This curry (without the cilantro leaves) even finds favor with children who normally adore tuna but are not so keen on curry sauces.

Tuna Curry with Coconut and Cilantro

Serves 6

If you do not like cilantro leaves, substitute flat-leaved French parsley.

3	cans (7 oz) of tuna in oil
2	leeks, trimmed and sliced thinly
1 inch	cube of gingerroot, peeled and finely sliced
5	large cloves garlic, peeled and sliced
1	small green chili, deseeded and finely sliced
2	medium green bell peppers, deseeded and sliced
3 tbsp	medium curry powder—check the ingredients to make sure there is no wheat or gluten
1½	cans (14 oz) of garbanzos, drained
1½	cans (14 oz) of coconut milk
	juice of 2–3 limes or lemons
2	handfuls of cilantro leaves, chopped

Drain the oil from the tuna into a heavy wide pan. Set the tuna aside. Add the leeks, gingerroot, garlic, chili, green pepper and curry powder and cook together for 3–4 minutes.

Add the garbanzos and coconut milk, bring to a boil and simmer covered for a further 10 minutes. Add the tuna fish and cook for a further 5 minutes.

Finally add the lime or lemon juice to taste and seasoning if it is needed.

Serve the curry, liberally sprinkled with the fresh cilantro, with lots of freshly cooked rice and a green salad.

PER SERVING	
Calories	337.38
Protein g	35.17
Fat g	12.54
Saturated fatty acids g	1.95
Monounsaturated fatty acids g	4.66
Polyunsaturated fatty acids g	6.80
Carbohydrate g	22.66
Total Sugars g	7.35
Sodium mg	605.45
Fiber g	7.08

It is surprising how well fruit goes with fish, both cooked and raw. Classic combinations such as mackerel and gooseberry, and salmon with apple, use the sharpness of the fruit to counteract the richness of the oily fish.

Salmon, Apple and Peanut Salad

Serves 4

A very quick and easy salad to make, it is given great texture by the combination of crunchy apple and peanut with the softness of the salmon.

1	can (14 oz) red salmon
2	medium-sized Granny Smith apples
4 oz	dry roasted peanuts
4 fl oz	homemade or good quality bought mayonnaise (check the ingredients list for wheat starch / gluten)
	juice of ½ large lemon
	pinch of salt
	freshly ground black pepper
	iceberg lettuce

Drain the salmon and flake it. Core and dice the apples but do not peel them. Mix the salmon in with the apples and peanuts. Thin the mayonnaise with the lemon juice and season to taste with salt and pepper. Toss the fish and apple mixture in the mayonnaise and adjust the seasoning to taste.

Arrange the lettuce on a serving dish and pile the fish mixture on top to serve.

PER SERVING	
Calories	503.48
Protein g	24.94
Fat g	41.40
Saturated fatty acids g	7.51
MonounSaturated fatty acids g	24.9
Polyunsaturated fatty acids g	8.33
Carbohydrate g	8.48
Total Sugars g	6.83
Sodium mg	698.31
Fiber g	2.51

Barbecue cooking is excellent for people with food allergies as long as they make sure that what they eat is cooked without any dressing apart from a little oil or salt and pepper. They can then easily use their own small side dish of dressing to spice up their barbecue.

Salmon en Papillotte

Serves 6

This dish started life at dinner parties in Victorian India where it could be made with any white fish and must have been very light and refreshing when compared to the heavy English fare that so many expatriots favored. If you prefer, you can substitute fillets of hake or halibut for the salmon.

6	salmon steaks
6 tbsp	olive or walnut oil
2 oz	finely chopped shallots
2	cloves garlic, finely chopped
	large handful of fresh parsley
3 tbsp	white wine vinegar
	grated peel of 2 limes
	pinch salt
	pepper

Put the fish in a microwave dish or flat pan, cover it with boiling water and simmer for 5 minutes on the stove or 2 minutes in a microwave. Drain carefully and set side.

Mix all the other ingredients thoroughly in a glass or porcelain dish large enough to hold the fish comfortably. Lay the fish on top of the marinade, then spoon over the excess to make sure the steaks are well immersed. Cover the dish and leave for 6–12 hours.

To cook the fish, lay the cutlets, with their marinade, on an ample bed of foil and cover them with well-oiled waxed paper. The fish can then be cooked on a barbecue, under a hot broiler or in a wide heavy frying pan. Cooking should take between 6 and 8 minutes, depending on the thickness of the steaks.

Serve with their marinade juices and lots of white rice and lightly cooked snow peas.

PER SERVING	
Calories	216.75
Protein g	8.21
Fat g	20.06
Saturated fatty acids g	3.10
MonounSaturated fatty acids g	12.69
Polyunsaturated fatty acids g	3.11
Carbohydrate g	1.07
Total Sugars g	.62
Sodium mg	173.52
Fiber g	.35

The mashed potato base for this recipe makes an excellent dish on its own. You could use it as a vegetable with a meat dish or salad, either hot or cold, or try serving it hot with grilled bacon or a poached egg perched on the top.

Edward Abbott's Shellfish Salad

Serves 6

Another fish dish from the outposts of the Victorian British Empire. This one comes from Edward Abbott, a very well traveled Tasmanian gourmet whose fascinating cookbook included lamb cooked with 17 oz of garlic cloves, as well as this salad.

1 lb	mashing potatoes
6	hard boiled egg yolks
4 tbsp	white wine vinegar
8 tbsp	olive oil
4 tsp	wholegrain mustard (check ingredients to make sure it does not contain gluten/wheat)
	salt
½ tsp	cayenne pepper
4 tbsp	milk
6	whole scallops
7 oz	crabmeat
4 oz	cooked squid, fresh or frozen
1	large head crisp lettuce
6	jumbo shrimp, fresh cooked or frozen
1	bunch watercress

Scrub and boil, or steam, the potatoes in their skins. Cool them slightly, then skin them and mash with the hard boiled egg yolks. Add the vinegar, olive oil, mustard, salt and cayenne, then reduce the purée with the milk and amalgamate the mixture thoroughly.

Simmer the scallops in a little white wine or water with a slice of lemon for 4–5 minutes or until they are cooked through. Set aside to cool.

Mix the crabmeat and squid into the potato mixture and adjust the seasoning to taste. Allow to cool completely. To serve, make a bed of lettuce on the serving dish. Pile the potato and seafood mixture in the middle and garnish with the scallops, shrimp and watercress.

PER SERVING	
Calories	458.78
Protein g	31.61
Fat g	30.60
Saturated fatty acids g	6.43
MonounSaturated fatty acids g	19.12
PolyunSaturated fatty acids g	3.95
Carbohydrate g	15.96
Total Sugars g	2.83
Sodium mg	760.67
Fiber g	1.71

Fresh beets are a greatly under-rated vegetable. They are deliciously flavored and especially excellent for pregnant mothers as they are high in fiber. Steam small beets until just cooked, then serve them with butter or olive oil and freshly grated sea salt.

Dutch Herring and Beet Salad

Serves 6

This salad has a real Nordic flavor of the sea. Great for summer lunches or picnics.

9 oz	baby beets, scrubbed
9 oz	new potatoes, scrubbed
6	pickled herring fillets
8 fl oz	plain low-fat yogurt
	large handful of chopped fresh parsley
	juice of 1 large lemon
	salt
	pepper

Steam the beets and potatoes until cooked, then cut the beets into match sticks and the potatoes into slices. Cut the herring fillets into thin match sticks.

Mix the fish, beets and potatoes in a bowl, add the yogurt and parsley and mix together until the fish and vegetables are thoroughly coated in the yogurt. Season to taste with the lemon juice, salt and pepper and serve with lots of fresh wheat- and gluten-free brown bread or rye-only pumpernickel (if you can eat rye).

PER SERVING	
Calories	194.95
Protein g	13.57
Fat g	7.86
Saturated fatty acids g	.64
MonounSaturated fatty acids g	.97
PolyunSaturated fatty acids g	.35
Carbohydrate g	18.06
Total Sugars g	11.63
Sodium mg	665.55
Fiber g	1.43

If you like a crunchy consistency to a crumble topping you can always spread some crushed potato chips over the top and brown them lightly under the broiler just before serving.

Fish Crumble

Serves 4

This simple fish crumble should appeal to adults and children alike, although you might want to leave the shrimp out of the children's version.

1 lb	haddock fillets
1	large onion, chopped roughly
8 oz	leeks, trimmed and sliced thickly
16 fl oz	milk
1 tbsp	butter or low-fat spread
1 tbsp	potato flour
4 oz	fresh or frozen shrimp
	salt and pepper
3 oz	rice flour
1 oz	corn flour or cornmeal
2 oz	butter or margarine
2 oz	strong flavored cheese, grated

Heat the oven to 350°F.

Put the fish, with the onion, leeks and milk into a pan or a microwave dish. Cover and cook on the stove for 10–15 minutes, or in a microwave on high for 8 minutes, or until the fish flakes easily.

Remove the fish carefully from the pan, discard any skin or bones and flake it coarsely. Strain the milk, reserving the onions and leeks. Melt the butter or spread in a clean pan (it will stick if you use the milky one) and add the potato flour. Mix well then slowly add the strained milk, stirring continually, and cook until the sauce thickens. Add the haddock, shrimp and vegetables and seasoning to taste. Spoon the mixture into an ovenproof casserole or pie dish.

Rub the butter or low-fat spread and grated cheese into the 2 flours until you have a crumble consistency; then spread it over the fish mixture. Bake for 30 minutes to cook and brown the crumble. Serve at once with a couple of green vegetables.

PER SERVING	
Calories	414.99
Protein g	23.13
Fat g	21.93
Saturated fatty acids g	9.48
MonounSaturated fatty acids g	8.39
PolyunSaturated fatty acids g	2.98
Carbohydrate g	25.94
Total Sugars g	5.48
Sodium mg	774.46
Fiber g	2.55

Okra is very popular in Caribbean cookery and adds a delicious subtle flavor to a sauce. However, you need to make sure that it is well cooked to get the best taste. It is not a vegetable that is improved by being served *al dente*.

Guyanan Okra with Shrimp

Serves 4

The idea for this recipe was given to me by Rosamund Grant whose Afro-Caribbean cookery books have made Caribbean cookery come alive for me.

4 tbsp	sunflower oil
1	medium onion, chopped
1	large clove garlic, chopped
7 oz	okra, topped, tailed and chopped
½	small green bell pepper, deseeded and sliced
½ tsp	paprika
½ tsp	ground cumin
1 tbsp	chopped fresh parsley
9 oz	fresh or frozen (thawed) shrimp
	salt
	pepper
2	medium-sized tomatoes, chopped

Cook the onion and garlic in the oil for a few minutes, and then add the okra and pepper and continue to cook for 7–10 minutes. Add the spices, herbs, shrimp and a little seasoning and go on cooking for a further 10–15 minutes. Finally, add the tomatoes, stir well, adjust the seasoning to taste and cook for a further minute or two to get the tomatoes well warmed through. Serve with boiled brown or white rice.

PER SERVING	
Calories	222.5
Protein g	14.11
Fat g	16.26
Saturated fatty acids g	2.33
MonounSaturated fatty acids g	3.83
PolyunSaturated fatty acids g	9.89
Carbohydrate g	5.71
Total Sugars g	4.55
Sodium mg	596.17
Fiber g	3.43

Frozen or even canned crabmeat work very well for this dish if you can not get fresh.

Crab Cobbler

Serves 6

This is a delicious dish for anyone who enjoys crabmeat but does not like having to struggle with the shell! It also reheats well.

2 tbsp	olive oil
4 oz	leeks, cleaned and very finely sliced
4 oz	fennel, cleaned and very finely sliced
4 oz	portobello mushrooms, chopped
1 tbsp	cornstarch
5 fl oz	milk
14oz	cooked crabmeat, brown and white mixed
2 tbsp	fresh sour cream or crème fraîche
	juice of 1 lemon
5 fl oz	medium sherry (optional)
3 oz	rice flour
3 oz	garbanzo (garbanzo/fava bean) flour
2 hpg tsp	wheat- and gluten-free baking powder
2 oz	butter
2 tbsp	freshly grated Parmesan
7 fl oz	buttermilk or soured milk
	sea salt
	freshly ground black pepper

Heat the oven to 350°F.

Heat the oil in a heavy pan and add the leeks and fennel. Cover and turn heat down really low; sauté for 15–20 minutes or until the vegetables are really soft. Add the mushrooms and continue to cook for a further 5 minutes. Add the cornstarch, stir for a minute or two and then gradually add the milk, stirring while the sauce thickens. Add the crabmeat, lemon juice and sherry and season to taste. Pour the mixture into an ovenproof casserole or pie dish.

Meanwhile, mix the flours with the baking powder and rub in the butter. Add the Parmesan and stir in the buttermilk until it reaches a soft dropping consistency.

Spoon the cobbler mixture over the crab mixture—it does not matter if it is not smooth—and bake in the oven for 30–35 minutes until the top is crisp and lightly tanned.

Ever Popular Fish Cakes

Serves 4

If your children prefer fish fingers, these cakes can just as easily be made into a finger shape.

14 oz	cod or haddock fillets
7 oz	mashing potatoes, scrubbed or peeled
3 tbsp	milk
1 tsp	butter
	salt
	black pepper
	juice of 1 lemon
2 tbsp	oatmeal, powdered in a food processor (or, if you are celiac and are dubious about oats, plain potato chips crushed very finely)
1 tbsp	sunflower oil

Steam, boil or microwave the potatoes until they are well cooked, then skin and mash them with the milk, butter and a little salt, pepper and lemon juice.

Bring the fish, just covered in water, to a boil in a microwave or in a pan and simmer for 4–5 minutes or until it is cooked. Remove from the water and flake or, if you like your fish cakes very smooth, purée in a food processor. Mix the fish thoroughly into the mashed potatoes and adjust the seasoning to taste.

Form the mixture into four large fish cakes and cover them thoroughly with the powdered oats or chips. Heat the oil in a wide pan and gently fry the fish cakes for about 8 minutes on each side or until they are nicely crisped.

They can be served alone or with a tomato sauce or gluten- and wheat-free ketchup.

Serve the fish cakes to the whole family so that everyone gets used to eating more wheat-free food. The chances are that they will not notice any difference!

PER SERVING	
Calories	234.28
Protein g	20.53
Fat g	9.34
Saturated fatty acids g	3.53
Monounsaturated fatty acids g	2.40
Polyunsaturated fatty acids g	2.98
Carbohydrate g	18.58
Total Sugars g	1.30
Sodium mg	217.05
Fiber g	1.52

Mussels are quick and easy to cook, quite cheap and many would say taste just as good as much more expensive oysters.

Paella

Serves 6

A classic Spanish dish—and excellent for those on a wheat- or gluten-free diet as neither wheat not gluten has any place in it. The recipe looks rather long and complicated but really is not—and well worth the little extra effort.

1 lb 2 oz	fresh mussels in their shells. You can also use 7 oz frozen mussels out of their shells although the flavor will not be quite as good
1 lb 2 oz	large shrimp or crayfish, fresh if possible but if not, frozen
4 tbsp	olive oil
1	medium onion, chopped finely
2	cloves garlic, chopped finely
1	large green bell pepper, deseeded and chopped
1	large tomato
1 tsp	paprika
6 1 tsp	saffron threads or ground saffron
	a few drops of Tabasco
4 oz	chorizo sausage, cut in thick slices
9 oz	monkfish fillets
1 lb 2 oz	short-grained brown or Arborio risotto rice
9 oz	fresh young peas, podded, or frozen peas
2 ¼ pints	water
	salt
2	handfuls of fresh parsley, chopped

Scrub the mussels thoroughly and remove any beards. Heat 2 inches of water in a large pan then toss in the mussels and let them steam for 5–6 minutes. Discard any that have not opened and set the rest aside, reserving the juices.

If you are using fresh crayfish or shrimp, boil them in 4 inches of lightly salted water for 6 minutes, then leave to cool in the water. Shell the seafood and reserve the water.

Heat the oil in a large heavy pan and gently fry the onion, garlic and pepper until they are soft but not colored. Chop the tomato into small pieces and add it to the pan. Continue to cook until the tomato has reduced down. Stir in the paprika, saffron and Tabasco. Add the juices from the mussels and shrimp and the chorizo sausage. Finally, add the monkfish cut into cubes, the rice, and the peas if you are using fresh. Pour in enough boiling water to cover the rice, then bring the paella back to a boil and simmer gently, uncovered, for 15–20 minutes or until the rice is cooked. Add more water if it looks as though it is drying up.

When the rice is done, add the shellfish (either the pre-cooked fresh or the frozen, defrosted), the frozen peas (if you are using frozen rather than fresh) and the parsley. Cover the dish loosely and allow to rest for 15 minutes. Adjust the seasoning before serving.

PER SERVING	
Calories	658.98
Protein g	43.75
Fat g	18.88
Saturated fatty acids g	4.24
MonounSaturated fatty acids g	10.52
PolyunSaturated fatty acids g	2.75
Carbohydrate g	78.3
Total Sugars g	5.39
Sodium mg	1065.23
Fiber g	3.29

Stir-fries are a wonderful way of creating a tasty supper from left-over vegetables. Quick and easy to cook, you can add flavor and nutrients with a few nuts or seeds added at the last moment.

Stir-Fried Artichokes with Tuna

Serves 4

A quick and spicy dish with a distinctly Chinese flavor. However, take care if you want to use any of the standard Chinese sauces (soy, hoisin, yellow bean, etc.) as most of them contain wheat starch.

3 tbsp	olive oil
3	fresh green chilies, carefully seeded and finely sliced
3	large cloves garlic, peeled and thinly sliced
6	green onions, trimmed and chopped
5 oz	fennel, trimmed and cut into matchsticks
14 oz	Jerusalem artichokes scrubbed and cut into matchsticks
1	can (15 oz) tuna, drained and flaked
2 tbsp	sunflower seeds
2 tbsp	mushroom ketchup
	black pepper
	fresh parsley, roughly chopped

Heat the oil in a large pan or wok and cook the chilies, garlic and green onions until they are lightly colored. Add the artichoke and fennel matchsticks and stir well for a couple of minutes. Add the tuna, well broken up, and the sunflower seeds. Cook uncovered for a minute or two, then reduce the heat, cover the pan and cook gently for around 15 minutes or until the artichoke is just cooked but still crisp. Add the mushroom ketchup and stir well to amagalmate—season with pepper. Add the parsley and serve at once with plenty of brown rice or wheat- and gluten-free noodles.

PER SERVING	
Calories	400.16
Protein g	27.77
Fat g	25.60
Saturated fatty acids g	4.71
PolyunSaturated fatty acids g	10.74
MonounSaturated fatty acids g	12.47
Carbohydrate g	17.42
Total Sugars g	3.50
Sodium mg	658.91
Fiber g	6.41

Pasta

Fresh Pasta

Sweet Pepper and Chicken Pasta Pie

Seafood Pasta

Sunflower and Cilantro Pesto

Curried Pasta and Sausage

Basic Tomato Sauce

Lasagne

Spaghetti with Smoked Salmon

Penne with Frankfurters and Greens

Pasta Primavera

Avocado and Bacon Salad

Spaghetti Bolognese

Pasta and Broccoli au Gratin

Pasta Rusticano

Tuna and Corn Macaroni

Frankfurter and Cheese Ravioli

*Vegetarian Pasta with Spinach
and Fava Beans*

Proprietary wheat- and gluten-free pastas can be excellent—we find that the rice pastas work especially well—but they are expensive and not always easy to find. Since they come dried, it would be worth keeping a stock in the larder for the day when you do not have the time or energy to make your own.

Fresh Pasta

Serves 4

If you cannot buy wheat- and gluten-free ready-made pasta, you will have to make your own. If you have an electric pasta maker this is very easy but electric pasta makers are quite expensive. However, even if you do not want to invest a lot of money, it would be worth buying a hand pasta maker which will at least save you the rolling and cutting, which used to take up so much of the Italian housewife's time.

7 oz	sifted garbanzo (garbanzo/fava bean) flour
2 oz	rice flour
2	medium eggs

If you have an electric pasta maker, put in the flours, then add the eggs according to the instructions. This mixture will work for spaghetti, tagliatelli, penne and lasagne sheets.

If you have a hand pasta maker, sift the flours together, make a well in the center, break in the eggs and gradually draw the latter into the flour and mix to a soft dough. Then feed the mixture through the pasta maker according to its instructions.

Leave the pasta to "rest" for at least 30 minutes; then cook in plenty of lightly salted boiling water for 4–6 minutes, depending on which shape and thickness of pasta you have made, and serve with the sauce of your choice.

PER SERVING	
Calories	246.35
Protein g	14.40
Fat g	6.04
Saturated fatty acids g	1.18
Monounsaturated fatty acids g	1.96
Polyunsaturated fatty acids g	1.71
Carbohydrate g	35.11
Total Sugars g	1.60
Sodium mg	62.13
Fiber g	5.60

Raw red bell peppers are immensely popular with children as a snack—and brimming with nutrients and vitamins. To tempt them first time round, cut the peppers in thin slices and mix them in with some yellow and a few green slices. I have never known it to fail!

Sweet Pepper and Chicken Pasta Pie

Serves 4

A cheerful and filling pie which will go down well with children and adults alike.

3 tbsp	olive oil
2	cloves garlic, finely chopped
1	large red bell pepper, deseeded and finely sliced
7 oz	cooked chicken, chopped small
2 tsp	dried oregano
10 fl oz	dry white wine or chicken stock
4 oz	plain yogurt
	salt
	pepper
9 oz	gluten- and wheat-free pasta shapes
2 oz	grated Parmesan cheese
1	small pack plain potato chips, crushed with a rolling pin

Heat the oil in a heavy pan and gently fry the garlic and pepper for a few minutes. Add the chicken, oregano and wine. Cover and simmer for 10 minutes. Add the yogurt and stir in well. Adjust the seasoning to taste.

Meanwhile, cook the pasta according to the instructions on the pack.

Put a layer of the filling in the bottom of a heat-proof dish. Cover this with the pasta and cover the pasta with the remains of the filling. Sprinkle the grated cheese and crushed potato chips generously over the top and brown lightly under a broiler for a few minutes. Serve at once.

PER SERVING	
Calories	586.95
Protein g	30.28
Fat g	23.34
Saturated fatty acids g	6.82
Monounsaturated fatty acids g	11.84
Polyunsaturated fatty acids g	3.16
Carbohydrate g	55.85
Total Sugars g	5.59
Sodium mg	373.60
Fiber g	3.21

For those people worried about their fat levels and too much heavy cream, soy milk manufacturers now make excellent soy creams that can be happily substituted for real cream in cooked dishes.

Seafood Pasta

Serves 4

This is a rather spectacular dish but it needs good organization as you must cook all three parts of the dish at the same time and serve it as soon as it is cooked to do it full justice.

10 ½ oz	wheat- and gluten-free noodles. Depending on which variety you use, you may need slightly more or slightly less as some "bulk up" more than others.
3 tbsp	sunflower oil
4 oz	leeks, trimmed and finely sliced
1	red chili, deseeded and finely sliced
2 tbsp	olive oil
4 oz	mussels without shells, fresh or frozen, but very well rinsed
1 tbsp	brandy
4 fl oz	heavy cream
2 lb 4 oz	fresh mussels in their shells
10 fl oz	dry white wine
	generous handful of parsley, finely chopped
	salt
	pepper

PER SERVING	
Calories	722.55
Protein g	43.07
Fat g	27.74
Saturated fatty acids g	8.88
Monounsaturated fatty acids g	9.63
Polyunsaturated fatty acids g	2.76
Carbohydrate g	65.67
Total Sugars g	6.44
Sodium mg	1669.42
Fiber g	3.04

Heat a large pan of lightly salted water to boiling point, then toss in the pasta. Cook it briskly according to the instructions on the pack until it is cooked but still *al dente*. Drain, add the sunflower oil and keep warm.

While the pasta is cooking put the leek and chili in a large pan with the oil and cook very gently until the vegetables are soft without being burned. Add the well-rinsed and dried shelled mussels to the leeks and heat through. Warm the brandy, pour it over the leeks and mussels, and flame it; then add the cream.

At the same time put the wine in a large pan with the parsley and bring it to a boil. When it is boiling hard, toss in the mussels in their shells and cook for 2–3 minutes or until all the shells have opened; if any do not open, discard them.

Add the mussels in shells and their cooking liquid to the previously flamed mixture. Season to taste.

To serve, pile the pasta in a large dish and spoon the seafood mixture with its juices over the top. Serve at once.

Prepared sauces for pasta are a boon to a busy cook, and there is no reason why being on a gluten- or wheat-free diet should change this. However, remember that they can be used not only with pasta but with potatoes, or even with rice, for a light supper dish.

Sunflower and Cilantro Pesto

Serves 4

This makes an interesting change from the standard basil and pine nut pesto—and it is very easy to make.

1 oz	fresh cilantro leaves
2 oz	sunflower seeds
2	large cloves garlic, peeled
4 tbsp	olive oil
	juice of 1 lemon
	salt
	pepper

Put all the ingredients in the bowl of a food processor and mix until they are well chopped and amalgamated. Take care not to process them too much or they will become too solid. Toss the cooked hot pasta in the sauce and serve with fresh Parmesan and freshly ground black pepper.

PER SERVING	
Calories	212.23
Protein g	3.04
Fat g	21.13
Saturated fatty acids g	2.82
Monounsaturated fatty acids g	11.86
Polyunsaturated fatty acids g	5.71
Carbohydrate g	3.09
Total Sugars g	.59
Sodium mg	99.76
Fiber g	.87

In this day of the microwave you can leave this dish sitting in the fridge and merely heat up a slice as needed.

Curried Pasta and Sausage

Serves 4

A hearty pasta dish for a cold evening.

9 oz	wheat- and gluten-free pasta shapes
1 oz	butter
2	small onions, peeled and finely chopped
1	large red bell pepper, deseeded and finely chopped
2 tbsp	curry powder (check to make sure it is wheat- and gluten-free)
7 oz	spicy Italian sausage (check ingredients to make sure they do not include any wheat/gluten)
1	can (14 oz) chopped tomatoes
	salt
	pepper
1 oz	apricot jam (optional)
5 fl oz	plain low-fat yogurt

Cook the pasta according to the directions on the pack; drain thoroughly.

Meanwhile, melt the butter in a large pan and gently cook the onions and bell pepper with the curry powder until the vegetables are softening. Add the sausage chopped up quite small and the tomatoes with most of their juice. Cook them all together until the flavors are well amalgamated and everything heated well through. If the sauce is very runny reduce it a bit by cooking it with the lid off the pan. Season to taste with salt and pepper and add the apricot jam.

Tip in the pasta and mix all well together and reheat. Turn into a serving dish and, just before serving, pour the yogurt over the top.

PER SERVING	
Calories	518.7
Protein g	16.4
Fat g	22.46
Saturated fatty acids g	5.11
Monounsaturated fatty acids g	3.31
Polyunsaturated fatty acids g	1.69
Carbohydrate g	67.07
Total Sugars g	17.86
Sodium mg	720.99
Fiber g	4.64

Basic Tomato Sauce

Serves 4

A useful basic tomato sauce for pasta—or indeed anything else !

1 lb	onions, finely chopped
3	large cloves garlic, finely chopped
3 lbs	ripe tomatoes, roughly chopped
1 tsp	sugar
	salt
	pepper

Put the onions in a heavy pan with the garlic, tomatoes and sugar. Bring slowly to a boil and simmer gently for 30–45 minutes or until the juices are considerably reduced. Season with salt and pepper. Liquidize and sieve the sauce if you want it smooth.

To vary the flavor, you can add a teaspoon of fresh or dried chopped herbs (almost any variety—but basil is particularly Italian), half a chopped dried chili, three finely chopped black olives or a couple of finely chopped anchovies—or anything else you fancy!

PER SERVING	
Calories	122.70
Protein g	4.34
Fat g	1.38
Saturated fatty acids g	1.50
Monounsaturated fatty acids g	1.54
Polyunsaturated fatty acids g	.87
Carbohydrate g	25.06
Total Sugars g	21.92
Sodium mg	134.70
Fiber g	5.48

For vegetarian children you could easily convert this into a veggie dish by substituting soy vegetable protein mix for the beef. However, you will need to increase the liquid by about half as soy absorbs much more liquid than real meat.

Lasagne

Serves 6

A classic lasagne, this both freezes and reheats well.

4 tbsp	olive oil
2	cloves garlic, chopped
2	medium onions, chopped
12 oz	ground beef
7 oz	mushrooms, sliced
2 tbsp	tomato purée
2	cans (14 oz) tomatoes
10 fl oz	red wine
1 tsp	dried thyme
4 oz	wheat- and gluten-free pre-cooked lasagne sheets
1 oz	butter
1 oz	potato flour
10 fl oz	milk
5 fl oz	white wine
4 tbsp	light cream
2 oz	ricotta or other crumbly white cheese
1	whole egg plus 1 egg yolk

Melt the oil in a large pan and gently fry the garlic and onion until they are beginning to soften. Turn up the heat, add the ground meat and fry it briskly for a couple of minutes. Reduce the heat again and add the mushrooms. Cook for about 5 minutes, then stir in the tomato purée, followed by the tomatoes, thyme and red wine. Bring to a boil and simmer gently, with the lid off, for 1–1 1/2 hours. Season to taste.

In an ovenproof dish, layer the Bolognese meat mixture with the pasta until both are used up, ideally starting and finishing with a meat layer.

Meanwhile, melt the butter in a pan, add the potato flour, cook for a few minutes, stirring continuously, then gradually add the milk, white wine and cream. Cook gently until the sauce thickens.

PER SERVING	
Calories	541.90
Protein g	22.38
Fat g	33.66
Saturated fatty acids g	14.40
Monounsaturated fatty acids g	17.49
Polyunsaturated fatty acids g	3.65
Carbohydrate g	27.19
Total Sugars g	10.35
Sodium mg	264.79
Fiber g	2.74

Pastas are effectively interchangeable, the only difference being their shape. So always feel free to use another variety if your pantry does not include the one specified in the recipe.

Add the cheese and continue to cook until it is melted. Remove the pan from the heat, stir in the eggs and season to taste with salt and pepper. Pour the sauce over the lasagne and bake it in a medium oven (350°F) for 30 minutes or until it is heated right through and the top is lightly tanned. Serve at once.

Spaghetti with Smoked Salmon

Serves 4

This recipe can be quite economical if you use the packaged smoked salmon offcuts which are now available in most supermarkets.

1 fl oz	olive oil
4 oz	button mushrooms, finely sliced
9 fl oz	dry white wine
1 hpg tsp	fresh dill, chopped or 1 tsp dried
	small handful of fresh chives, chopped or 2 hpg tsps dried
10 fl oz	light cream
9 oz	smoked salmon, cut into thin matchsticks
	juice of 1 lemon
9 oz	gluten- and wheat-free spaghetti
	salt
	pepper

Heat the oil in a wide pan and gently fry the mushrooms for 4–5 minutes; do not let them color. Add the wine, increase the heat and cook fast for a further 5 minutes to reduce the wine. Add the herbs and the cream, mix thoroughly, then add the salmon and reheat gently but do not boil or the sauce will curdle.

Season to taste with salt, pepper and lemon juice. Cover, set aside and keep just warm.

PER SERVING	
Calories	502.02
Protein g	28.87
Fat g	18.55
Saturated fatty acids g	5.75
Monounsaturated fatty acids g	8.97
Polyunsaturated fatty acids g	2.75
Carbohydrate g	48.54
Total Sugars g	4.24
Sodium mg	1331.5
Fiber g	2.13

Although pasta is eaten throughout the country, Italian cooking varies enormously from the mountains in the north to the hot, flat plains of southern Italy. This dish would find no favor in Naples !

PER SERVING	
Calories	602.04
Protein g	24.71
Fat g	34.73
Saturated fatty acids g	4.84
Monounsaturated fatty acids g	9.73
PolyunSaturated fatty acids g	2.42
Carbohydrate g	51.08
Total Sugars g	8.73
Sodium mg	8902.36
Fiber g	6.09

Meanwhile, cook the pasta according to the instructions on the pack until it is just *al dente*. Drain and rinse thoroughly with boiling water.

Turn the pasta into a warmed serving dish and gently mix in the salmon sauce before serving.

Penne with Frankfurters and Greens

Serves 4

Based on a northern Italian recipe, this is a hearty but flavorsome dish that goes down well with children—even though it does contain cabbage!

7 oz	wheat- and gluten-free pasta, penne or macaroni
3 tbsp	olive oil
7 oz	onions, finely chopped
14 oz	loose-leafed green cabbage, shredded
7 fl oz	vegetable stock
4	frankfurters (check to make sure they contain no starch or gluten), sliced into rounds
2 oz	fresh Parmesan cheese, grated

Cook the penne or macaroni according to the instructions on the pack until it is just *al dente*, then drain. Meanwhile, gently fry the onions in the oil until they start to soften but have not colored. Add the cabbage greens and stock, cover and cook for 5 minutes or until the greens are starting to soften.

Slice the frankfurters into rounds, add to the greens and continue to cook for a further 5 minutes to allow the flavors to amalgamate. You should not need any further seasoning. Mix in the pasta, reheat and turn into a serving dish.

Grate the Parmesan over the dish and mix in well. Serve at once.

Certain canned vegetables (artichokes, legumes such as chick peas or beans, sweet corn, water chestnuts and olives are my favorites) are invaluable to have in your pantry. No matter how little else you may have, combined with rice or even on their own they make an excellent and quick meal.

Pasta Primavera

Serves 4

A quick and easy pasta dish. To make it vegetarian or vegan, leave out the ham and replace the cream with soy cream.

3 tbsp	sunflower oil
2	medium leeks, finely sliced
4	sticks celery, finely chopped
4 oz	mushrooms, finely sliced
7 oz	canned artichoke hearts, drained and quartered
2 oz	chopped ham
5 oz	light cream
10 fl oz	dry white wine
	juice of 1 lemon
	salt
	pepper
1 lb	wheat- and gluten-free pasta shapes of your choice
	handful of fresh parsley, chopped

Heat the oil in a heavy pan and gently cook the leek and celery until soft; add the mushrooms and continue to cook for a few minutes. Add the artichoke hearts and the ham, then the cream and the wine. Mix well and allow to simmer for a few minutes. Add the lemon juice and season to taste. Set aside to keep warm.

Cook the pasta in plenty of fast-boiling water according to the instructions on the pack until it is just cooked or *al dente*. Drain the noodles quickly and turn them into a dish. Stir the parsley into the sauce, spoon it over the noodles and serve at once.

PER SERVING	
Calories	666.31
Protein g	19.97
Fat g	23.52
Saturated fatty acids g	8.30
MonounSaturated fatty acids g	7.56
PolyunSaturated fatty acids g	9.36
Carbohydrate g	88.11
Total Sugars g	7.82
Sodium mg	286.81
Fiber g	5.38

Avocados are always difficult to judge and so disappointing if they are rock hard. Some varieties get darker as they ripen, and when they are black they are ready to eat.

Avocado and Bacon Salad

Serves 4

A more elegant version of the ever-popular avocado and bacon sandwich—excellent for lunch or a substantial starter.

2 tbsp	olive oil
2	medium leeks, peeled and finely sliced
6	slices of lean back bacon
5 oz	gluten/wheat-free pasta shells
1	large ripe avocado
2 oz	pine nuts, lightly crushed
	about 20 leaves of fresh basil
	juice of 1 large lemon
	salt
	freshly ground black pepper

Heat the oil in a heavy pan and gently cook the leeks for 10–15 minutes until they are quite soft.

Grill the bacon slices briskly until they are tanned and crisp on both sides. Dry them off on some paper towels to remove any excess grease and chop them into small pieces.

Meanwhile, cook the pasta in plenty of lightly salted boiling water until it is *al dente*. How long this will take will depend on the type of pasta (rice or corn based) that you are using. Drain it and tip it into a serving bowl. Dribble over some of the olive oil and mix well.

Carefully core, peel and dice the avocado.

Amalgamate the leeks, bacon and avocado with the pasta, mixing it gently to avoid damaging the avocado pieces.

Add the pine nuts, chopped basil leaves, lemon juice and salt and pepper to taste.

Serve at once as a starter or light luncheon salad.

PER SERVING	
Calories	609.48
Protein g	17.02
Fat g	48.87
Saturated fatty acids g	12.97
Monounsaturated fatty acids g	23.76
Polyunsaturated fatty acids g	10.19
Carbohydrate g	27.73
Total Sugars g	3.42
Sodium mg	1128.68
Fiber g	5.70

It is a good idea to make two or three times the amount of sauce that you need and freeze the extra in small containers, ready for use at a moment's notice.

Spaghetti Bolognese

Serves 6

The addition of chicken livers not only adds a depth of flavor to this recipe but increases one's intake of Vitamin A.

1 tbsp	olive oil
3 oz	lean bacon slices
1	medium onion, finely chopped
1	medium carrot, finely chopped
1	small stick celery, finely chopped
9 oz	lean ground beef
4 oz	chopped chicken livers
2 tbsp	tomato purée
4 fl oz	dry white wine
7 fl oz	water or vegetable stock
	salt, pepper and nutmeg
10 oz	wheat- and gluten-free spaghetti

Heat the oil in a heavy, deep pan and gently brown the bacon. Add the onion, carrot and celery and continue to cook until they are brown. Add the beef and turn regularly so that it browns evenly. Add the chicken livers, then, in a couple of minutes, the tomato purée and white wine. Season lightly with the salt, pepper and a pinch of nutmeg and add the stock or water. Cover the pan and simmer very gently for 30–40 minutes.

Meanwhile, cook the spaghetti according to the instructions on the pack.

To serve, mix the sauce well into the pasta and serve at once.

Pass around some grated Parmesan cheese if you like.

PER SERVING	
Calories	412.43
Protein g	19.46
Fat g	18.73
Saturated fatty acids g	5.94
Monounsaturated fatty acids g	8.02
Polyunsaturated fatty acids g	1.43
Carbohydrate g	41.72
Total Sugars g	4.29
Sodium mg	332.46
Fiber g	2.41

If you want to make this dish more "adult" you could add a handful of whole blanched almonds to the sauce before mixing in the pasta and broccoli.

Pasta and Broccoli au Gratin

Serves 4

A more filling version of a classic broccoli with cheese sauce. Very popular with children !

5 oz	wheat- and gluten-free pasta shapes
10 oz	broccoli florets
1	medium onion, chopped very roughly
1 oz	butter
1 oz	potato flour
10 fl oz	milk
4 fl oz	dry white wine
7 oz	sharp Cheddar cheese, grated
1 oz	wholegrain mustard (check that it is wheat- and gluten-free)
	salt
	pepper

Cook the pasta according to the instructions on the pack, drain and keep warm.

Cook the broccoli and onion in a steamer until they are just cooked but still slightly *al dente*. Save the water from steaming.

Meanwhile, heat the butter in a pan and add the potato flour. Slowly add the milk and wine and continue to heat, stirring continuously, until the sauce thickens. Add three-quarters of the cheese and the mustard, then season to taste. If the sauce is a bit thick, thin it with a few spoonfuls of the water from the broccoli.

Gently mix the pasta into the broccoli and onion, then spoon both into a warmed casserole or pie dish. Spoon over the sauce and sprinkle the remaining cheese over the top and brown under the broiler. Serve at once.

PER SERVING	
Calories	511.56
Protein g	24.40
Fat g	27.33
Saturated fatty acids g	16.59
MonounSaturated fatty acids g	7.64
PolyunSaturated fatty acids g	1.79
Carbohydrate g	40.60
Total Sugars g	7.62
Sodium mg	586.81
Fiber g	4.13

Do not be tempted to buy mini vegetables instead of young ones. They may look pretty but they have very little flavor.

Pasta Rusticano

Serves 4

A good pasta dish when there are vegetarians around. You can successfully serve it to both meat eaters and abstainers !

2	young carrots, sliced in thin rounds
2	sticks celery, diced
1	medium onion, peeled and chopped roughly
1	large zucchini, sliced in rounds
2	cloves garlic, sliced thinly
1 tsp	dried marjoram
2 tsp	dried oregano
1	can (14 oz) tomatoes
4 oz	dry white wine
7 oz	canned or frozen fava beans, or fresh young fava beans, cooked for 5 minutes in lightly salted water
	salt
	pepper
7 oz	gluten- and wheat-free pasta (brown rice macaroni works very well in this dish)
3 oz	freshly grated Parmesan

Put the carrots, celery, onion, zucchini, garlic and herbs in a heavy pan with the tomatoes and the white wine. Bring to a boil, cover and simmer for 10–15 minutes or until the carrots and celery are just cooked but still slightly crunchy. Add the fava beans and season to taste with salt and pepper. Continue to cook for another few minutes to warm the beans through.

Meanwhile, boil the pasta in plenty of lightly salted water until just *al dente*, then drain and keep warm.

Carefully fold the pasta into the vegetables and serve at once, heavily sprinkled with Parmesan.

PER SERVING	
Calories	353.97
Protein g	15.10
Fat g	7.19
Saturated fatty acids g	5.45
Monounsaturated fatty acids g	3.86
Polyunsaturated fatty acids g	1.61
Carbohydrate g	52.55
Total Sugars g	7.28
Sodium mg	471.86
Fiber g	5.30

You could make this in individual bowls to be stored in the refrigerator so that you could heat it up for individual family members when they are hungry.

Tuna and Corn Macaroni

Serves 4

Another great success for adults and children as it combines three favorite foods—pasta, corn and tuna—although you may need to leave the parsley out for some !

7 oz	gluten- and wheat-free macaroni
4 tbsp	sunflower oil
5 oz	button mushrooms, sliced
1 oz	potato flour
18 fl oz	milk
7 oz	canned sweetcorn niblets, drained
7 oz	canned tuna fish, drained and flaked
	juice of 1 large lemon
	salt
	pepper
2	large handfuls of parsley, chopped

Cook the pasta according to the instructions on the pack until just *al dente*; drain and keep warm.

Heat the oil in a heavy pan and gently cook the mushrooms for 5 minutes. Add the potato flour, stir well, then gradually add the milk. Bring back to a simmer and cook until the sauce thickens. Add the corn and tuna fish and mix well. Season to taste with the lemon juice, salt and pepper, then mix in the pasta. If necessary, thin the sauce with a little extra milk. Just before serving, stir in the parsley.

PER SERVING	
Calories	560.03
Protein g	28.22
Fat g	27.33
Saturated fatty acids g	6.05
Monounsaturated fatty acids g	6.59
Polyunsaturated fatty acids g	13.16
Carbohydrate g	54.35
Total Sugars g	9.77
Sodium mg	488.96
Fiber g	6.71

Since I have never yet come across a gluten- and wheat-free ravioli, this is something that you really may have to make for yourself. However, take heart as it really is not very difficult. If you are nervous, make sure that you have plenty of sauce to pour over the top. Even if the ravioli fall to pieces they will taste good.

Frankfurter and Cheese Ravioli

Serves 6

Surprisingly easy to make, these ravioli are really tasty. If you find them a little dry on their own or just with oil, you could serve them with the tomato sauce on page 55.

13 oz	fresh pasta (see page 50) made into lasagne sheets
4	frankfurters (check ingredients to ensure they do not include wheat or gluten)
3 oz	Cheddar cheese, cut into very thin slivers
4 tbsp	olive oil
2 oz	freshly grated Parmesan

Lay out the freshly made lasagne sheets on a floured board. Halve them, then cut both halves into 12 large or 18 smaller squares.

Cut the frankfurters into 1-inch lengths, then cut them in half down their length. Lay out the frankfurters on the squares of pasta and cover them with the slivers of cheese. Brush the edges of the squares with water, then cover them with the other squares of pasta. Press the edges down firmly. Place the ravioli on a plate, cover with damp kitchen paper and leave in the fridge for at least half an hour.

Heat a large pan of lightly salted water. When it is boiling gently, lift the ravioli in with a slotted spoon. Simmer them gently for 4–5 minutes or until the pasta is cooked. Remove to a heated serving dish, dribble with the olive oil, sprinkle with the Parmesan and some freshly ground black pepper and serve at once.

PER SERVING	
Calories	407.23
Protein g	18.39
Fat g	26.88
Saturated fatty acids g	6.61
MonounSaturated fatty acids g	10.24
PolyunSaturated fatty acids g	2.51
Carbohydrate g	24.20
Total Sugars g	1.40
Sodium mg	444.77
Fiber g	3.76

Vegetarian Pasta with Spinach and Fava Beans

Serves 6

This dish will be good for vegetarians—as well as everyone else. It is simple, quick and easy.

1 tbsp	cornstarch
1tbsp	tomato purée
7 fl oz	tomato juice
8 oz	frozen leaf spinach, drained
1	can (7 oz) fava beans
8 oz	firm tofu, cut into small dice (you can use a smoked tofu if you prefer a smoky flavor, but check the ingredients on the pack)
	salt, pepper and nutmeg to taste
12 oz	gluten- and wheat-free pasta of your choice

Mix the cornstarch with the tomato purée, then add the tomato juice to make a smooth purée. Heat slowly, stirring continually, till the sauce thickens. Add the spinach, fava beans and tofu, mix well, and season to taste with the salt, pepper and nutmeg.

Cook the pasta in plenty of fast-boiling water according to the instructions on the pack. Reheat the sauce gently and serve spooned over the pasta.

PER SERVING	
Calories	322.00
Protein g	10.10
Fat g	6.03
Saturated fatty acids g	0.80
MonounSaturated fatty acids g	3.25
PolyunSaturated fatty acids g	1.98
Carbohydrate g	56.70
Total Sugars g	8.15
Sodium mg	453.00
Fiber g	4.80

Poultry and Meat

Coq au Vin Blanc

Turkey with Artichoke Hearts and Orange Sauce

Chicken Satay

Chicken Breasts Braised with Noodles and Mushrooms

Chicken Kiev

Chicken Nuggets

Lemon Chicken in Batter with Lemon Sauce

Chicken Breasts with Coconut Milk

Chicken Breasts Stuffed with Smoked Salmon

Chicken Rosti

Chicken and Asparagus Pie

Chicken with Okra, Chili and Bananas

Chicken Risotto with Fennel and Pine Nuts

Chili Pancakes

"Battered" Meat Loaf

Paprika Beef with Brandy and Cream

Corn and Beef Hash Pie

Beef Crumble

Roast Beef, Italian Style

Steak and Kidney Pie

Cassoulet

Spring Lamb en Croûte

Fidget Pie

Rack of Lamb with Mustard Crust

Curried Lamb with Yogurt

Bobotie (Lamb and Lentil Casserole)

Leg of Lamb Casserole with Beans and Spinach

Leg of Lamb with Zucchini and Butter Beans

Alternative Moussaka

Pork Sausages with Oatmeal (not for celiacs)

Pork Sausages with Polenta

Ham and Chicory-Stuffed Pancakes

Sweet and Sour Pork

Pork Fillet with Jerusalem Artichokes and Orange

Cauliflower in Cheese Sauce with Bacon and Green Peas

Pheasant Braised with White Grapes

Duck with Apple and Orange Sauce

If you cannot get button onions, you could use pickling onions, although they are very difficult to peel. If neither are available, use 1 large Spanish onion, chopped roughly.

Coq au Vin Blanc

Serves 6

A white version of the classic French dish, the white wine gives a slightly lighter texture to the sauce without losing any of its flavor.

1 tbsp	butter
2 tbsp	olive oil
4 oz	unsalted lean bacon, diced
20	button onions
2	cloves garlic, finely chopped
8 oz	button mushrooms, washed and dried
6	chicken parts, breasts or legs, as you prefer
1 oz	lightly seasoned potato flour
2	bouquet garni
6 tbsp	water
20	baby new potatoes
3 tbsp	brandy
7 fl oz	full-bodied, but not sweet, white wine—Muscadet is quite good
1/2 oz	soft butter
1/2 oz	potato flour
	large handful of fresh parsley, chopped

Heat the oven to 350°F.

Melt the butter and oil in a heavy casserole and briskly fry the bacon, onions and garlic until they are beginning to soften. Add the mushrooms and continue to cook until the vegetables are all golden but not burned. Remove them with a slotted spoon and keep them warm. Toss the chicken parts in the seasoned flour and sauté them in the same casserole until they too are golden on both sides.

Return the vegetables to the casserole, add the bouquet garni and the water, cover the casserole and bake it in the oven for 30–40 minutes or until the chicken is really tender.

Meanwhile, steam or boil the potatoes until cooked, drain them and keep them warm.

PER SERVING	
Calories	450.15
Protein g	36.57
Fat g	20.92
Saturated fatty acids g	7.30
Monounsaturated fatty acids g	11.31
Polyunsaturated fatty acids g	2.84
Carbohydrate g	20.91
Total Sugars g	3.75
Sodium mg	401.47
Fiber g	2.34

If you buy your turkey on the bone rather than off, you can make an excellent stock from the bones with a few vegetables. If you add a little rice or a few lentils to the stock, simmer it for half an hour and season it to taste, you will have an instant and low-cost soup.

When they are done, remove the chicken and vegetables from the casserole, arrange them on a serving dish with the potatoes and keep them warm.

Skim as much extra fat off the casserole juices as possible. Warm the brandy in a ladle, pour it onto the juices and light it. Let it burn for a minute or two, then pour on the wine. Stir thoroughly to make sure you get any burned bits off the bottom of the casserole, then cook briskly for 5–10 minutes to reduce the quantity slightly.

Mix the softened butter with the potato flour and add it, in small pieces, to the sauce. Continue to cook until the sauce thickens. Adjust the seasoning to taste, then pour the sauce over the chicken and vegetables.

Sprinkle liberally with the chopped parsley and serve at once.

Turkey with Artichoke Hearts and Orange Sauce

Serves 6

Now that it is easy to buy turkey pieces rather than the whole bird, it can be eaten every day, not just at Thanksgiving. If you do not like the slightly stronger taste of the turkey, you can use the recipe with chicken breasts.

1 lb 9oz	boneless turkey fillets
2 tbsp	olive oil
2	onions, very finely sliced
7 oz	celery, chopped small
½ oz	potato flour
8 oz	artichoke hearts, freshly cooked, or frozen or canned and drained
	rind and juice of 4 oranges
	salt
	pepper

Put the turkey pieces with an extra onion and carrot and approximately 1 pint of water in a pan and bring them slowly to a boil. Simmer gently for 25–30 minutes or until the meat is just cooked, and then remove the turkey and strain and reserve the stock.

PER SERVING	
Calories	214.15
Protein g	28.83
Fat g	7.15
Saturated fatty acids g	2.81
MonounSaturated fatty acids g	5.84
PolyunSaturated fatty acids g	1.92
Carbohydrate g	11
Total Sugars g	8.09
Sodium mg	205.27
Fiber g	1.10

Because of the publicity given to peanut allergy these days many people are avoiding peanuts altogether. However, as long as you do not have an allergy to them they are extremely nutritious, not to mention delicious. Very useful for a wheat- or gluten-allergic person to carry with them in case they feel hungry when nothing else wheat- and gluten-free is available.

Meanwhile, heat the oil in a pan and slowly cook the onions and celery until they are soft but not colored. Add the potato flour then, gradually, 15 fl oz of the reserved stock, the rind and juice of two of the oranges and the artichoke hearts. Cook all together for a couple of minutes until the sauce has thickened, then add the turkey pieces, heat the dish through thoroughly and season to taste with salt and pepper.

Transfer it into a warmed serving dish and decorate with the remaining two oranges, neatly segmented, before serving with rice or new potatoes and a green vegetable.

Chicken Satay

Serves 6

This popular Eastern dish can be served either as a main course with rice or on little sticks as a cocktail or buffet dish. In the latter case, pass around a dish of the sauce with the satay sticks—plus some napkins !

6	boneless chicken breasts
1 oz	ground almonds
1 tbsp	shredded gingerroot
1 tsp	ground coriander
1 tsp	ground turmeric
1 tsp	sugar (raw cane)
10 fl oz	coconut milk
2 tbsp	sunflower oil
½ tsp	chili powder
9 oz	onions, very finely chopped
8 oz	peanut butter (check ingredients list for wheat or gluten)
1 tsp	sugar
1 tbsp	mushroom ketchup (check ingredients list for wheat or gluten)
	juice of ½ a lemon or lime

PER SERVING	
Calories	733.35
Protein g	49.26
Fat g	55.25
Saturated fatty acids g	12.54
MonounSaturated fatty acids g	25.35
PolyunSaturated fatty acids g	15.76
Carbohydrate g	10.93
Total Sugars g	8.46
Sodium mg	338.44
Fiber g	3.65

Heat the oven to 350°F.

Mix the almonds, ginger, spices and 1 teaspoon sugar. Add the coconut milk, mix well, then use this to marinate the chicken breasts for about 2 hours. Transfer the breasts, with the marinade, to an oven-proof dish, cover and bake for 40 minutes. Meanwhile, heat the oil in a pan with the chili powder and sauté the onions until they are quite soft. Take off the heat and add the peanut butter and all the other ingredients to taste.

Meanwhile, cook plenty of brown or white rice to accompany the satay.

When the chicken is done, remove it from the oven, add the cooking juices to the sauce mixture, adjust the seasoning to taste and spoon over the chicken before serving with a good green salad and lots of rice. If serving as a cocktail snack, cut chicken into bite-size pieces and thread on to sticks.

Chicken Breasts Braised with Noodles and Mushrooms

Serves 4

This dish can be made with chicken breasts or legs, depending on whether you prefer dark or light meat. Even though it is a bore, it is worth skinning the tomatoes.

4 tbsp	olive oil
2 oz	leeks, trimmed and sliced thinly
7 oz	zucchini, topped, tailed and sliced thickly
5 oz	tomatoes, peeled (dunk in boiling water for 1 minute then peel off skin) and chopped
4	chicken breasts, skin removed
4 oz	field mushrooms, thickly sliced
7 oz	gluten- and wheat-free noodles
	sea salt
	freshly ground black pepper

Heat 2 tablespoons of the oil in a heavy pan and add the leeks. Cook briskly for a couple of minutes, then add the sliced zucchini.

PER SERVING	
Calories	411.85
Protein g	17.25
Fat g	18.23
Saturated fatty acids g	3.10
PolyunSaturated fatty acids g	2.47
MonounSaturated fatty acids g	12.49
Carbohydrate g	43.28
Total Sugars g	2.34
Fiber g	1.38
Sodium mg	256.51

A real party dish that few people are prepared to tackle at home although it is not that difficult as long as you do not try to rush the chiling of each operation.

Continue to cook for another few minutes before adding the tomatoes. Turn the heat down, place the chicken portions on top of the vegetables and cover the pan. Simmer gently for 30 minutes or until the chicken is cooked, then adjust the seasoning to taste.

Meanwhile, heat the remaining oil in a small pan and cook the mushrooms lightly.

Cook the noodles briskly in plenty of fast-boiling water for 3–4 minutes, drain briefly, and mix with the mushrooms. Serve the chicken with its vegetables, accompanied by the mushrooms and noodles.

Chicken Kiev

Serves 4

The secret to keeping the butter inside the chicken breast is to chill the breast well between each stage of preparation.

4 oz	butter
4	cloves garlic, crushed
	large handful of fresh parsley, chopped fine
	good squeeze of fresh lemon juice
4	chicken breasts
4 oz	cornflakes, crushed
1½ oz	potato flour
2	large eggs, beaten

Soften the butter thoroughly, add the garlic, parsley and a squeeze of lemon juice and beat well. Divide into 4 portions, shape into rectangles and put in the freezer for at least an hour.

With a sharp knife, split the breasts in half horizontally but do not cut all the way through. Open them out flat on wet waxed paper. Cover with more wet waxed paper, then beat them flat with a rolling pin.

Put the cornflakes in a plastic bag and crush them thoroughly with a rolling pin—they should be almost powdered—then mix with the potato flour.

Place one piece of the seasoned butter on each breast and then roll the breast so that the butter is sealed inside. Roll each breast in the egg and then in the cornflake mixture. Chill in the refrigerator

PER SERVING	/
Calories	501.49
Protein g	32.75
Fat g	29.43
Saturated fatty acids g	16.26
MounounSaturated fatty acids g	8.8
PolyunSaturated fatty acids g	2.18
Carbohydrate g	28.74
Total Sugars g	3.08
Sodium mg	612.88
Fiber g	1.17

for 30 minutes. Take out and repeat the egg and "breadcrumbing," then return to the refrigerator for another 30 minutes.

Meanwhile, heat the oven to 350°F.

Place the chicken breasts on a rack over a baking sheet, and bake in the oven for 20–30 minutes or until the crust is crisp and tanned and the breasts are cooked.

Remove carefully onto a heated serving dish and serve at once with a selection of green vegetables.

Although intended for children, these nuggets can also be used as a cocktail snack with a dipping sauce.

Chicken Nuggets

Serves 6

You can substitute plain potato chips for the cornflakes for these nuggets or use the batter in the recipe for Lemon Chicken on page 74.

7 oz	cornflakes
2 oz	potato flour
1 lb 5oz	lean chicken meat, cubed or diced into whatever size nuggets you need
2	eggs, beaten
	vegetable oil for deep frying

Crush the cornflakes as small as you can by putting them into a plastic bag and rolling them with a rolling pin. Turn them into a flat dish and add the potato flour, mixing well.

Roll the chicken cubes in the beaten egg. Then roll the nuggets in the cornflake mixture until they are completely coated. Set them aside in a covered dish, in the fridge, for an hour or so.

Heat the oil in a deep pan or a deep fryer until a piece of stale bread turns brown in 1 minute.

Deep fry the nuggets for approximately 7 minutes or until the coating is crisp and lightly browned and the middle is cooked but not dried up. Drain on paper towels and serve at once.

PER SERVING	
Calories	432.58
Protein g	26.54
Fat g	21.75
Saturated fatty acids g	3.63
Monounsaturated fatty acids g	8.18
Polyunsaturated fatty acids g	8.41
Carbohydrate g	35.13
Total Sugars g	3.15
Sodium mg	481.73
Fiber g	.78

Do not use ordinary bread cubes when testing the heat of the oil as they could contaminate the oil with a tiny amount of gluten.

Lemon Chicken in Batter with Lemon Sauce

Serves 4

The lemon in this recipe gives it a real tang. You can make all the parts in advance so that you only have to deep-fry the chicken breasts before you serve them.

4	chicken breasts
15	coriander seeds, lightly crushed
	small pinch salt
2	grinds black pepper
	grated rind and juice of 2 lemons
4 oz	sifted garbanzo (garbanzo/fava bean) flour
16 fl oz	water
	small pinch salt
1 oz	butter
1	heaping tsp potato flour
	vegetable oil for deep frying

Marinade

Lay out the chicken breasts in a flat dish. Cover them with the crushed coriander seeds and a light sprinkling of salt and pepper. Pour over the juice of the 2 lemons. Cover and leave for at least 1 hour.

Batter

Make the batter by processing the sifted flour, a small pinch of salt, the lemon rind and 7 fl oz of the water in a food processor.

Lemon sauce

Remove the chicken breasts and set aside. Strain the marinade into a small saucepan, add the butter and melt slowly. Add the potato flour, stir well, then gradually add the remaining water. Bring to a boil and cook gently until the sauce thickens. Keep warm.

To serve

Heat the oil in a large pan or deep fryer until a small piece of stale gluten- and wheat-free bread turns brown in 1 minute.

Dip the chicken breasts in the batter and make sure they are well covered. Gently lower each breast into the oil and cook fairly gently for 5 minutes. Increase the heat under the oil and continue to cook the breasts until their batter is crisp and tanned. Remove

PER SERVING	
Calories	270.91
Protein g	30.90
Fat g	11.34
Saturated fatty acids g	4.89
Monounsaturated fatty acids g	3.99
Polyunsaturated fatty acids g	2.15
Carbohydrate g	13.50
Total Sugars g	1.20
Sodium mg	246.65
Fiber g	2.75

and drain briefly on paper towels. Serve at once with the lemon sauce.

Since fresh coriander is sometimes difficult to get, you can always substitute fresh parsley. The flavor will be different but still good. This would be better than using dried coriander leaf which really needs long cooking to bring out its flavor.

Chicken Breasts with Coconut Milk

Serves 6

A delicious low-calorie, low-fat chicken dish with a strong hint of the Far East.

2 tbsp	olive oil
7 oz	leeks, trimmed and very finely sliced
7 oz	fennel, trimmed and very finely sliced
6	cooked chicken breasts
7 oz	fresh spinach, chopped (or frozen leaf spinach, defrosted)
1½ pints	coconut milk
1 oz	potato flour
	handful of fresh coriander leaves, chopped
	juice of 1–2 fresh limes
	salt
	white pepper

Heat the oil in a wide, heavy pan, add the leeks and fennel, cover and sauté gently for 15–20 minutes or until the vegetables are quite soft. Add the chicken breasts with the spinach. Mix the potato flour with a little of the coconut milk to make a smooth paste, then add that, along with the rest of the coconut milk.

Cover the pan again and continue to cook gently until the chicken breasts are cooked through and the sauce has thickened slightly. Add the coriander, chopped, the lime juice and salt and pepper to taste. Serve at once with plenty of basmati rice and a salad or a green vegetable such as snow peas.

PER SERVING	
Calories	210.57
Protein g	22.5
Fat g	8.09
Saturated fatty acids g	2.1
MonounSaturated fatty acids g	6.52
PolyunSaturated fatty acids g	2.92
Carbohydrate g	12.92
Total Sugars g	8.79
Sodium mg	373.32
Fiber g	3.58

Chicken Breasts Stuffed with Smoked Salmon

Serves 4

These chicken breasts are also good cold, in which case let them get quite cold before removing them from the parcels. Slice with a very sharp knife and serve with a salad.

4 tbsp	olive oil
9 oz	leeks, trimmed
5	cloves of garlic, peeled and thinly sliced
5 oz	short-grain white rice or risotto rice
1¾ pints	water or unsalted vegetable stock
1 oz	sun-dried tomatoes, chopped
1 lb 2oz	celeriac, peeled and diced
3½ oz	smoked salmon pieces
4	chicken breasts

Warm half the oil in a heavy pan and add half the leeks and 3 of the garlic cloves. Cook gently for about 5 minutes or until they are just softened. Add the rice, stir around for a few minutes, then add the water. Bring to a boil and simmer briskly for 15–20 minutes or until the water is absorbed and the rice is soft.

Meanwhile, put the rest of the oil into a deep casserole dish with the rest of the leeks and garlic, the tomatoes, celeriac and 3 or 4 tablespoons of the water or stock. Bring to a boil and simmer for 5–10 minutes.

Put 4 tablespoons of the rice mixture into a bowl and mix in the smoked salmon pieces.

Lay the chicken breasts out on a flat surface, cover them with wet waxed paper and beat them flat with a mallet. Remove the waxed paper and use half of the rice to cover two of the chicken breasts. Top them with the other chicken breasts. Lay out 2 new muslin cloths and place one of the chicken breast parcels on each. Fold the corners up to make a loose parcel so that the stuffing does not fall out in the cooking.

Carefully lift the two parcels and put them on top of the simmering vegetables. Cover the casserole and simmer for 35–45 minutes or until the chicken is quite cooked and the celeriac soft.

Carefully remove the two parcels from the pan, let them rest for about half an hour and then untie them. Gently reheat the

PER SERVING	
Calories	465.63
Protein g	34.58
Fat g	20.83
Saturated fatty acids g	3.35
MonounSaturated fatty acids g	11.93
PolyunSaturated fatty acids g	3.89
Carbohydrate g	34.06
Total Sugars g	3.87
Sodium mg	708.5
Fiber g	6.26

You can also use these potatoes on their own as a vegetable to go with a roast of meat—or just as a crunchy supper dish.

remaining rice. With a very sharp knife, slice the chicken breasts thickly into 4–6 slices. Lift carefully onto the serving dish or plates and serve with a spoonful of the remaining rice and the vegetables with their juices.

You could also serve a green vegetable such a broccoli or a green salad.

Chicken Rosti

Serves 4

An unusual version of a favorite Swiss grated-potato dish.

4	boned chicken breasts
3½ oz	Gruyère cheese, sliced
1 lb 2oz	baking potatoes, scrubbed
7 oz	onions

Heat the oven to 350°F.

Open up the chicken breasts horizontally, like a book. Divide the cheese equally inside each breast. Fold over the breast to make a square parcel and set aside.

Grate the scrubbed potatoes coarsely (you can leave their skins on) and slice the onion thinly. Mix the two together. Place the four breasts in the bottom of a large baking dish (ideally one from which you can serve) and spread the potato and onion mixture over them. Cover lightly with a piece of foil and bake for 20 minutes. Remove from the oven, remove the foil and mix the potatoes around slightly if their edges look as though they are getting burned. Then return to the oven for a further 20 minutes to crisp the top of the potatoes.

Serve at once with a green vegetable or salad.

PER SERVING	
Calories	444.00
Protein g	27.63
Fat g	26.38
Saturated fatty acids g	12.85
PolyunSaturated fatty acids g	3.73
MonounSaturated fatty acids g	11.68
Carbohydrate g	25.70
Total Sugars g	3.80
Fiber g	2.33
Sodium mg	247.75

Chicken and Asparagus Pie

Serves 6

This is an excellent pie for a cold summer lunch or supper although it also tastes good hot. If you wish to economize you could use asparagus pieces rather than tips.

3 lb 5 oz	whole chicken
2	onions, chopped
2	carrots, chopped
4 oz	margarine
3 oz	rice flour
5 oz	garbanzo (garbanzo/fava bean flour
5 tbsp	water
2 oz	cornstarch
4 fl oz	homemade chicken stock / water
4 fl oz	dry white wine
4 fl oz	whole milk
1	can (14 oz) asparagus spears, drained
4 fl oz	heavy cream
	sea salt
	black pepper

Roast the chicken in a moderate oven for 45–60 minutes or until it is quite cooked. Remove from the oven, cool slightly then remove the flesh from the bones, tear it into small pieces and set aside.

Put the bones in a large saucepan with the chopped onions and carrots and 3–4 pints of water. Bring to a boil and simmer for 1–1½ hours; then drain off the stock and set aside 3½ fl oz of it. The rest can be used for soup.

Meanwhile, rub the margarine into the mixed rice and flour. Add approximately 5 tablespoons of water to make a soft (but not sticky) dough. Cover and leave it to rest in the fridge.

Mix the cornstarch with a little of the 3½ fl oz of stock to make a smooth paste, then add the rest of the stock, the white wine and the milk. Gradually bring to a boil over a slow heat, stirring constantly to prevent lumps.

Open the asparagus and drain off the liquid. Add this to the sauce along with the chicken pieces and the cream. Bring back to a boil and season to taste with salt and pepper. Finally, add the asparagus tips, taking care to mix them in gently so they do not get broken.

Spoon the mixture into a pie dish.

Roll the pastry out carefully until it is quite a bit larger than the pie dish. It should be quite thick to hold together.

Place the pie dish on the pastry and "cut out" a pie dish shape. Then cut out a border the width of the pie dish rim from the scraps. Wet the rim of the pie dish and line it with the cut out scraps. Wet the top of the pastry border then carefully, using a spatula and a rolling pin, lift the pastry top onto the top of the pie. Press the edges down with your thumbs, and use the scraps to decorate the top of the pie.

Cook it in a moderately hot oven–350°F—for 20–25 minutes until the pastry is crisp and lightly browned.

The pie can be served at once with hot vegetables. Alternatively you can let it cool to room temperature and serve it with a salad.

PER SERVING	
Calories	491.83
Protein g	32.92
Fat g	24.11
Saturated fatty acids g	8.87
Monounsaturated fatty acids g	7.58
Polyunsaturated fatty acids g	3.53
Carbohydrate g	34.16
Total Sugars g	3.17
Sodium mg	3195.79
Fiber g	4.87

Half a banana, mashed or finely chopped, makes an excellent addition to many meat casserole dishes as it gives them a richness of taste and texture without actually making them taste of banana.

Chicken with Okra, Chili and Bananas

Serves 4

A very Caribbean recipe—as good to cool you down on a hot summer evening as to warm you up on a cold winter's night.

4 tbsp	olive oil
1	large red bell pepper, deseeded and sliced
7 oz	okra, topped, tailed and sliced across, thickly
1	small fresh or dried red chili
14 oz	boneless raw chicken, breast or leg, cubed
1 lb	tomatoes, chopped roughly
	pinch ground coriander
1	large banana
	salt
	black pepper

Heat the oil in a pan and briskly fry the pepper and okra until both are softening. Add the chili and the cubed chicken and continue

PER SERVING	
Calories	411.03
Protein g	22.51
Fat g	30.14
Saturated fatty acids g	6.31
MonounSaturated fatty acids g	18.11
PolyunSaturated fatty acids g	4.84
Carbohydrate g	14.14
Total Sugars g	13.17
Sodium mg	282.05
Fiber g	4.19

You could also try using a red rice for this dish. You can get it in delicatessens or health food stores and it is deliciously nutty.

to fry briskly until the chicken is lightly browned all over. Add the tomatoes and coriander, cover the dish and cook over a very low heat for 25 minutes or until the chicken is cooked. If you cook it too quickly the tomatoes will dry up and you will need to add a little water or white wine.

Once the chicken is cooked, add the banana (peeled and sliced thickly), cook for a couple of minutes, then adjust the seasoning to taste. Serve hot with lots of brown rice and a really good green salad.

Chicken Risotto with Fennel and Pine Nuts

Serves 4

This is an excellent way to use up either cooked chicken or turkey. If you do not like cilantro, substitute flat-leaved French parsley.

2 tbsp	olive oil
2	sticks celery, chopped small
9 oz	fennel, chopped small
1	large red bell pepper, deseeded and sliced thinly
7 oz	brown rice
16 fl oz	water
5 fl oz	dry white wine
7 oz	cooked chicken
2 tbsp	pine nuts
	salt
	black pepper
2	sprigs fresh cilantro

Heat the oil in a heavy pan and add the celery, fennel and pepper. Cook gently until they are beginning to soften and then add the rice. Stir for a minute or two before adding the liquid. Bring to a boil and simmer, uncovered, for 15 minutes. Add the turkey or chicken and continue to cook until the liquid is almost evaporated

PER SERVING	
Calories	456.80
Protein g	21.42
Fat g	19.43
Saturated fatty acids g	3.48
Monounsaturated fatty acids g	10.22
Polyunsaturated fatty acids g	7.54
Carbohydrate g	46.08
Total Sugars g	5.85
Sodium mg	65.28
Fiber g	3.90

If you want to give this dish a Mexican feel, serve it with corn tortillas.

and the rice cooked; add a little more water if necessary. Add the pine nuts and seasoning to taste. Serve warm or cold, generously sprinkled with the chopped cilantro.

Chili Pancakes

Serves 4

This pancake recipe is good for any savory pancake   and makes for a very filling meal stuffed with chili con carne !

3 ½ oz	garbanzo (garbanzo/fava bean) flour
	salt
7 fl oz	water
1 tbsp	sunflower oil
1	medium onion, chopped
1	medium carrot, scrubbed and diced
2	small red chilies, deseeded and finely chopped
8 oz	ground beef
2 oz	potato flour
1 hpg tsp	cayenne pepper
3	medium tomatoes, roughly chopped
2 tbsp	tomato purée
16 fl oz	beef or vegetable stock
1	can (15 oz) red kidney beans, drained
	salt
	black pepper

Mix the flour, salt and water in a food processor, then allow it to stand for 10–15 minutes. You can either make 8 medium-sized, thin pancakes or four larger, thick ones. Choose your pan accordingly, then heat a small dribble of oil, just enough to cover the base, and cook the pancakes briskly on either side. Set them aside, inter-layered with plastic wrap.

Heat the oil in a pan and briskly fry the onion, carrot and chilies until they are lightly colored.

Increase the heat and add the meat; fry it rapidly until it is browned, then reduce the heat and add the potato flour mixed with the cayenne pepper. Stir for a few minutes before adding the tomatoes, tomato purée and the stock. Bring to a boil and simmer for 15–20 minutes. Add the beans and simmer for a further 5 minutes; then adjust the seasoning to taste.

With a slotted spoon, remove the meat, vegetables and beans from the pan and use them to fill the pancakes; place them in a serving dish. Reduce the remaining sauce in the pan slightly by boiling it briskly for 4–5 minutes; pour it over the pancakes and serve.

PER SERVING	
Calories	389.05
Protein g	27.00
Fat g	11.73
Saturated fatty acids g	3.49
MonounSaturated fatty acids g	4.22
PolyunSaturated fatty acids g	3.93
Carbohydrate g	46.88
Total Sugars g	9.99
Sodium mg	703.65
Fiber g	11.60

A really easy meal for kids when they come home from school—filling and tasty.

"Battered" Meat Loaf

Serves 6

A good old-fashioned way of using up a roast. The "battered" refers to the delicious cheesey batter which is poured over the loaf and makes a crispy crust.

1	egg yolk
2 oz	sifted garbanzo (garbanzo/fava bean) flour
4 fl oz	water
12 oz	cooked beef
5 oz	Cheddar cheese
1 tbsp	olive oil
1	medium onion, roughly chopped
1/2	large cooking apple, peeled and diced
1 oz	oatmeal (leave out if you are celiac)
1 tbsp	wholegrain mustard (check ingredients for wheat and gluten)
1 tsp	ground allspice
2	eggs

2 tbsp	low fat yogurt
	salt and pepper

Beat the egg yolk, flour and water in a food processor or mixer to make a batter and set aside.

Meanwhile, chop the meat reasonably finely in a processor or mincer and mix it with 4 oz of the cheese. Fry the onion in the oil until it is lightly browned and add to the meat mixture along with the apple, oatmeal, mustard and allspice. Mix the eggs with the yogurt and mix well into the meat; season lightly.

Form the mixture into a loaf shape on a baking sheet or an oven-proof serving dish. Beat half the remaining cheese into the batter and spoon half of the batter over the loaf. Bake it in a moderately hot oven (375°F) for 15 minutes. Remove from the oven, spoon over the rest of the batter, sprinkle the remaining cheese on top and return to the oven for another 15 minutes or until the top is nicely browned. Meanwhile, the extra batter will have dripped down the side and made a crunchy layer around the loaf. The loaf is good either hot or cold.

PER SERVING	
Calories	329.85
Protein g	29.88
Fat g	18.74
Saturated fatty acids g	8.26
MonounSaturated fatty acids g	7.88
PolyunSaturated fatty acids g	1.59
Carbohydrate g	11.57
Total Sugars g	4.26
Sodium mg	370.18
Fiber g	1.98

If you wanted to prepare this dish well in advance for a party you could cook it to the point where you need to add the snow peas and cream and freeze at that point. When you need to use it, defrost it at room temperature and complete the recipe.

Paprika Beef with Brandy and Cream

Serves 6

A rather rich dish for special occasions; the snow peas give it a lovely crunch.

2 tbsp	olive oil
2	medium onions, finely chopped
2	cloves garlic, crushed
1 oz	seasoned potato flour
2 tsp	paprika
2 lb 4 oz	lean braising beef, well trimmed of fat and cubed
2 tbsp	brandy
1 tsp	dried thyme
2	bay leaves
7 oz	tomatoes, peeled and chopped roughly
10 fl oz	dry white wine
7 oz	fresh snow peas, halved
	salt and pepper
4 fl oz	heavy cream

Heat the oil in a large pan and gently cook the onion and garlic until they are soft but not colored. Mix the paprika with the seasoned potato flour and toss the beef cubes thoroughly in it. Add the meat to the onion and garlic and fry briskly until lightly colored all over.

Remove from the heat and cool slightly, then add the brandy and light it. Once the flames have died, add the herbs, tomatoes and the wine making sure that you scrape any burned bits off the bottom of the pan. Bring to a boil, cover and simmer gently for 40–50 minutes or until the beef is really tender.

Remove the bay leaves, add the snow peas and continue to cook for a couple of minutes to just take the rawness off the snow peas (they should still be slightly crunchy). Add the cream and adjust the seasoning to taste. Serve at once, decorated with the bay leaves, accompanied by lots of brown rice or baked potatoes.

PER SERVING	
Calories	471.85
Protein g	51.65
Fat g	20.78
Saturated fatty acids g	8.78
MonounSaturated fatty acids g	10.25
PolyunSaturated fatty acids g	1.36
Carbohydrate g	9.87
Total Sugars g	4.97
Sodium mg	161.34
Fiber g	1.87

Even when cooking for children you can use wine in a casserole as by the time the meat is cooked the alcohol has also been cooked out of the wine just leaving its flavor behind.

Corn and Beef Hash Pie

Serves 6

A good filling family pie that goes down well with children.

1 lb 2oz	lean ground beef
2	medium onions, finely chopped
1	handful fresh parsley, chopped
2 tsp	dried mixed herbs
2 oz	oatmeal (leave these out if you are celiac)
	salt and pepper
4 fl oz	red wine
4 fl oz	water
1 tbsp	Worcestershire sauce
1 lb	sweet corn, frozen (defrosted) or canned (drained)
1	medium green bell pepper, chopped finely
4	green onions, finely chopped
1	egg, beaten
3 oz	sifted garbanzo (garbanzo/fava bean) flour
3 oz	rice flour
3 oz	margarine
3–4 tbsp	water

In a bowl, mix the beef, onions, herbs and oatmeal and season them lightly. Add the wine, water and Worcestershire sauce and mix thoroughly. Spread half the mixture in the bottom of a pie dish.

Meanwhile, mix the corn with the peppers and green onions and half the egg; spread this over the beef mixture. Top with the rest of the meat mixture. Cover the dish with foil or a lid and cook for 30 minutes in a moderate oven (350°F) or for 10 minutes in a microwave. Remove and cool slightly.

Rub the margarine into the flours until they resemble breadcrumbs and then mix to a soft dough, adding the water. Roll out the pastry and top the pie. Decorate with the trimmings, brush with the rest of the egg and return it to a slightly hotter oven (375°F) for 25–30 minutes or until the pastry is cooked and golden. Serve with a salad or green vegetables.

PER SERVING	
Calories	481.20
Protein g	26.07
Fat g	23.11
Saturated fatty acids g	8.14
MonounSaturated fatty acids g	10.37
PolyunSaturated fatty acids g	3.08
Carbohydrate g	41.23
Total Sugars g	5.51
Sodium mg	286.87
Fiber g	5.00

You can use this savory crumble topping with any other filling you may have.

Beef Crumble

Serves 6

Some people find pastry very time consuming to make so here is a recipe that gives you a topping to your beef pie without having to make the pastry !

2 tbsp	sunflower oil
4	medium leeks, washed and sliced thinly
1 lb	rutabaga, peeled and diced
1½ oz	seasoned potato flour
1 lb 5oz	lean stewing steak, well trimmed of fat and diced
10 fl oz	homemade beef or vegetable stock or water
4 fl oz	red wine
1	bouquet garni
	salt and pepper
4½ oz	sifted garbanzo (garbanzo/fava bean) flour
4½ oz	rice flour
2 oz	butter or margarine
2 oz	grated Cheddar cheese

Heat the oil in a pan and cook the leeks and rutabaga fairly briskly until they are lightly tanned all over. Toss the beef in the seasoned flour, then add it to the pan and continue to cook until the beef is brown. Add the stock and wine, stir around well, add the bouquet garni and cook very slowly in a moderate oven (350°F) for 1 hour or until the beef is really tender. Adjust the seasoning to taste and turn into a pie dish.

Rub the butter or margarine and cheese into the flours as for a pastry, and when they are well mixed spread the mixture over the beef. Put the dish into the oven for a further 30 minutes to cook and crisp the topping. Serve at once with a green vegetable.

PER SERVING	
Calories	454.48
Protein g	33.47
Fat g	17.9
Saturated fatty acids g	6.22
MonounSaturated fatty acids g	7.04
PolyunSaturated fatty acids g	5.44
Carbohydrate g	37.85
Total Sugars g	5.97
Sodium mg	291.36
Fiber g	5.92

Long, slow cooking will give flavor to any dish. A slow cooker, if you enjoy well flavored casseroles, might be a good investment.

Roast Beef, Italian Style

Serves 8

A splendid Victorian beef dish to serve for a dinner party. The bacon and the long slow cooking give the beef an excellent flavor.

2 oz	mushrooms, chopped very finely
2	handfuls of fresh parsley
½	medium onion, finely chopped
	freshly ground black pepper
2	thick slices of lean bacon
6 lb 8oz	round of beef
1 oz	butter
½ tsp	dried marjoram
½ tsp	dried thyme
	grated peel of 1 lime or small lemon
1	clove garlic, crushed
1	medium onion, finely chopped
4 oz	carrot, diced finely
2 tbsp	tomato purée
1 pint	water or homemade beef, veal or vegetable stock
8 oz	wheat- and gluten-free macaroni
1 tbsp	finely grated Cheddar cheese

Heat the oven to 300°F.

Mix the chopped mushrooms, parsley, onion and pepper and coat the slices of bacon. Cut an incision the length of the beef, lay in the coated bacon and tie the meat back into shape. Heat the butter in a heavy pan large enough to hold the beef and gently cook the herbs, peel, garlic, onion and carrot for 10 minutes. Place the meat on top of the vegetables. Mix the tomato purée with the stock and pour around the meat. Cover and cook very slowly in the oven for 3 hours.

When you are ready to serve the meat, cook the macaroni according to the instructions on the pack. Drain it thoroughly and return it to the pan. Remove the meat onto a large warmed serving

PER SERVING	
Calories	641.15
Protein g	93.20
Fat g	19.63
Saturated fatty acids g	8.84
Monounsaturated fatty acids g	8.18
Polyunsaturated fatty acids g	1.75
Carbohydrate g	24.87
Total Sugars g	3.33
Sodium mg	542.92
Fiber g	1.95

Try the steak and kidney pie cold with salad. Although cold meat pies have rather gone out of fashion they were great favorites with our grandparents—who knew a thing or two about good food.

dish and remove its ties. Adjust the seasoning of the cooking juices to taste and add them, along with the vegetables and the grated cheese, to the macaroni. Mix all well together and spoon it around the beef. To serve, slice the beef and serve it with the macaroni and vegetables.

Steak and Kidney Pie

Serves 6

An old British favorite often off the menu for wheat- and gluten-allergic people. The pie freezes well in its dish topped with pastry, either cooked or uncooked; if the latter take care not to burn the pastry when reheating it.

5 oz	sifted garbanzo (garbanzo/fava bean) flour
3 oz	margarine
1 lb 10 oz	stewing steak, well trimmed and cubed
1 lb	kidney, trimmed and diced
12 oz	button mushrooms, rinsed, dried and halved if they are very large
2 oz	potato flour
	salt and pepper
	water
1	egg

Heat the oven to 350°F.

Rub the margarine into the flour until it is crumbly, then mix to a paste with approximately 3 tablespoons water. Set aside in the fridge.

Mix the trimmed, cubed steak with the kidney and the mushrooms. Season the potato flour well, then toss the meats and the mushrooms in the flour until all the pieces are well covered. Turn them into a pie dish, sprinkle over any remaining flour and fill the dish 2/3 of the way up with cold water. Cover the dish with foil or a lid and cook it for about 1 hour or until the steak is tender. Take it out of

PER SERVING	
Calories	464.12
Protein g	46.22
Fat g	23.15
Saturated fatty acids g	8.21
MonounSaturated fatty acids g	10.51
PolyunSaturated fatty acids g	3.05
Carbohydrate g	19.1
Total Sugars g	1.15
Sodium mg	537.4
Fiber g	3.79

the oven after half an hour and stir to make sure that the flour is well mixed in.

Roll out the pastry and top the pie (supporting the middle with an egg cup if the dish is rather large for the filling), decorate the top with the pastry trimmings and brush with the beaten egg.

Return to the oven for 25–30 minutes or until the crust is cooked and lightly browned. The pie can be eaten hot with vegetables or cold with baked potatoes and a salad.

Cassoulet

Serves 6

Another classic and substantial dish normally barred to those allergic to wheat or gluten. Make sure you push the bread slices well down into the casserole so that they absorb the juices.

12 oz	dried kidney beans
4	slices of lean bacon
2	carrots, scrubbed and sliced
2	onions stuck with 10 cloves
4	cloves garlic, halved
10	peppercorns
	salt
1 oz	butter
6 oz	garlic sausages, diced
1 lb	leg or shoulder of lamb, trimmed of fat and cubed
2	large onions, chopped roughly
2 tbsp	tomato purée
25 fl oz	water or homemade chicken or vegetable stock
2	slices of gluten- and wheat-free white or wholemeal bread
2 tbsp	wholegrain or French mustard (check ingredients list for wheat and gluten)

Soak the beans in cold water for a minimum of 4 hours, then drain and discard the water. Line a casserole big enough to hold all the ingredients with the bacon slices. In a bowl, mix together the beans, carrots, onions stuck with cloves, 2 cloves of garlic, the peppercorns and salt. Spoon this mixture into the casserole with the bacon, just cover it with water and bake it, covered, in a moderately cool oven (325°F) for 2 hours.

Meanwhile, melt the butter in a heavy pan and brown the garlic sausage and the lamb. Stir in the chopped onion, the rest of the garlic, the tomato purée and the stock. Bring to a boil and simmer gently for 30 minutes.

Turn the meat mixture into the vegetable casserole, stir all well together and return to the oven for another 30 minutes. Taste and adjust the seasoning if necessary.

Spread the pieces of bread on one side with the mustard. Lay them on top of the casserole, mustard side up, and push them down so that the bottom of each slice absorbs the juices. Return the casserole to the oven for 20–25 minutes to heat and crisp the topping.

Serve at once with plenty of green vegetables or a salad.

PER SERVING	
Calories	542.64
Protein g	38.19
Fat g	30.26
Saturated fatty acids g	13.68
Monounsaturated fatty acids g	13.62
Polyunsaturated fatty acids g	2.91
Carbohydrate g	31.44
Total Sugars g	9.67
Sodium mg	945.5
Fiber g	6.17

Even though it is almost impossible to buy anything other than lamb these days—mutton is an endangered species—there is still something rather special about the first young lambs around Easter. Well worth a special effort.

Spring Lamb en Croûte

Serves 6

The garbanzo flour makes a delicious but crumbly pastry. When it goes in the oven the sides may "slither" down to the base leaving your *en croute* with a hat rather than totally covered but it looks quite attractive and tastes delicious.

5 oz	garbanzo (garbanzo/fava bean) flour
3 oz	margarine or butter
2 lb 4oz	boned and rolled leg or shoulder of lamb
4	cloves garlic, peeled but left whole
3 tbsp	olive oil
4 oz	button mushrooms, chopped finely in a food processor
3/4 oz	sun-dried tomatoes, soaked if necessary, and chopped finely
	large handful of fresh parsley, finely chopped

Put the flour into a bowl and cut in the margarine or butter. Crumble with your fingers until the mixture is like fine sand and then add about 4–6 tablespoons water to make a soft dough. Cover and put in the fridge to chill.

Cut three or four slits in the lamb and insert the garlic. Cover the lamb with a piece of foil and bake in a moderate oven (350°F) for 40 minutes. Remove and allow to partially cool.

Meanwhile, heat the oil and gently sauté the mushrooms with the sun-dried tomatoes, covered, for 10–15 minutes. Add the finely chopped parsley.

To finish, reheat the oven to 350°F. Roll out the pastry to a large enough square to cover the lamb.

Spread the mushroom mixture over the top of the lamb and then carefully cover the lamb, tucking the pastry in around the bottom of the joint. Decorate with spare scraps of pastry.

Return to the oven and bake for 20–25 minutes or until the pastry is crisp and lightly browned. Serve at once with lots of fresh vegetables.

PER SERVING	
Calories	544.44
Protein g	38.36
Fat g	37.94
Saturated fatty acids g	13.15
MonounSaturated fatty acids g	17.24
PolyunSaturated fatty acids g	4.72
Carbohydrate g	13.37
Total Sugars g	.99
Sodium mg	241.75
Fiber g	3.20

The combination of apples, onions and meat is a very familiar one in English cookery. A Devon Fidget Pie for example uses ham instead of lamb or mutton but is in other respects very similar to this one.

Fidget Pie

Serves 6

The Fidget Pie is quite sweet because of the apples and the cider but the sweetness complements the meat. You will be unlikely to find a fillet of mutton around these days but you should be able to find some reasonably mature lamb.

1 tbsp	sunflower oil
1	large onion, peeled and sliced
5 oz	cooking apple, peeled, cored and sliced
1 lb	mature lamb, trimmed of fat and cubed
½ oz	sugar (raw cane)
2 tsp	dried thyme
5 fl oz	dry cider
6 oz	garbanzo (garbanzo/fava bean) flour
3 oz	butter
	water
1	egg
	salt and pepper

Heat the oven to 350°F.

Pour the oil into the base of a round or oval pie dish and lay half the onion mixed with half the apple in the bottom. Trim the meat and cut it into 1 inch cubes. Season it well and mix it with the thyme and the sugar. Lay the meat over the apples and onions and cover it with the rest of the apple and onion mixture. Pour in the cider and cover the pie with foil.

Bake it for around 40 minutes or until the lamb is nearly cooked. Transfer to a smaller dish or put a pie support in the middle of the dish.

Meanwhile, make the pastry by rubbing the butter into the flour until it is sandy, then mixing to a soft dough with two or three tablespoons of water.

When the filling is ready, roll out the pastry. Cut a rim of pastry to go round the pie dish. Wet the rim of the dish with a little water to make the pastry stick, then wet the pastry rim to make the lid stick. Cover the pie, pressing down the edges with your fingers. Decorate the lid with the pastry trimmings (in balls or leaves) and brush generously with the beaten egg. Bake for 30 minutes or until the pastry is cooked and golden. Serve hot or warm with new potatoes and a green vegetable.

PER SERVING	
Calories	416.74
Protein g	29.8
Fat g	23.59
Saturated fatty acids g	12.29
MonounSaturated fatty acids g	7.03
PolyunSaturated fatty acids g	3.23
Carbohydrate g	21.63
Total Sugars g	7.19
Sodium mg	256.68
Fiber g	3.75

A rack of lamb is also excellent cooked on a barbecue. If you wish to do that, place the lamb on a branch of fresh rosemary which will not only flavor the lamb but scent it.

Rack of Lamb with Mustard Crust

Serves 6

The mustard crust gives an excellent flavor to the lamb. Serve with fresh green vegetables such as broccoli, spinach or green beans.

	Rack of lamb with at least 12 chops, trimmed of most fat
Crust	
1 tbsp	sunflower oil
4 tbsp	wholegrain mustard—check to make sure it does not contain wheat starch or gluten
1 oz	finely chopped parsley
4 oz	shallots, very finely chopped
1 tbsp	dried rosemary
1 tsp	dried marjoram
1 tsp	dried oregano
1 tsp	dried thyme
3 tbsp	dry white wine
1	small pack plain potato chips

Heat the oven to 350°F.

Roast the rack of lamb uncovered in a baking pan for 15 minutes per pound—this will give a moderately pink middle. If you want it well done, cook it for 20 minutes per pound.

Meanwhile, combine all the crust ingredients apart from the chips; crush these in a plastic bag with a rolling pin.

About 10 minutes before the meat is ready, take it out of the oven and spread the fat side with a thick layer of the mustard mixture. Sprinkle over the crushed chips and return it to the oven for the last 10 minutes to finish cooking the meat and crisp the crust.

PER SERVING	
Calories	305.45
Protein g	29.48
Fat g	18.00
Saturated fatty acids g	6.91
MounanSaturated fatty acids g	6.60
PolyunSaturated fatty acids g	3.00
Carbohydrate g	5.40
Total Sugars g	1.50
Sodium mg	294.11
Fiber g	1.18

This curry mixture also works well with pork or chicken.

Curried Lamb with Yogurt

Serves 6

Like most curries the flavor will mature if you can make the dish the day before you want to eat it, leave it in the fridge overnight then reheat it to serve. If you intend to do this, do not add the yogurt until just before serving the dish.

2 tbsp	sunflower oil
2	medium onions, peeled and finely chopped
3	large cloves garlic, peeled and finely chopped
1 oz	gingerroot, peeled and finely chopped
1 hpg tsp	ground cumin
6 hpg tsp	medium curry powder (check to make sure it does not contain any wheat or gluten)
7 oz	zucchini, topped and tailed and sliced
4 oz	green beans, topped and tailed and sliced
14 oz	tomatoes, fresh (peeled and quartered) or canned (chopped)
14 oz	cooked lamb trimmed of any fat and diced
14 fl oz	water
7 oz	cooking apples, peeled, cored and diced
2 oz	raisins
	juice of 2 large lemons
3½ fl oz	Marsala or medium sherry
7 oz	yogurt
	salt and black pepper

PER SERVING	
Calories	315.85
Protein g	17.89
Fat g	18.32
Saturated fatty acids g	7.47
Monounsaturated fatty acids g	6.98
Polyunsaturated fatty acids g	4.28
Carbohydrate g	17.48
Total Sugars g	14.62
Sodium mg	172.45
Fiber g	3.61

Heat the oil in a large, deep pan and add the onion, garlic, ginger-root and spices. Cook them all together gently for 5–10 minutes and then add the vegetables, the cooked lamb, the apple and the water. Bring to a boil and cover and simmer very gently for 30–40 minutes. Add the raisins, lemon juice and Marsala or sherry and continue to cook, scarcely even simmering for a further 10 minutes. Finally, add the yogurt and season to taste. Serve with plenty of rice and a green salad.

Bobotie (Lamb and Lentil Casserole)

Serves 6

This is a classic South African dish which, in the original, uses breadcrumbs with the lamb. However, lentils make an excellent substitute. It can be eaten hot or cold.

2 lb 4oz	1 medium-sized lean leg of lamb
3 ½ oz	brown lentils
1 pint	milk
2 tbsp	olive or sunflower oil
2	medium onions, chopped
2 tbsp	medium curry powder
	juice of 2 lemons
	salt and pepper
3	medium eggs
7 fl oz	milk
2 oz	chopped almonds
3 oz	raisins

Put the leg of lamb into a heavy ovenproof casserole with the brown lentils and the milk. Cover the pot tightly and bake in a moderate oven (350°F) for approximately 1 hour or until the lamb and lentils are cooked and most of the milk absorbed.

Remove the lamb from the casserole dish, remove the meat from the bones and mince it in a food processor. Mix the minced lamb with the lentils and any remaining milk.

Meanwhile, heat the oil in a heavy pan and add the onions and curry powder. Cook them together gently for around 5 minutes and then mix them into the lamb and lentils along with the lemon juice and a little seasoning. Spoon this mixture into an ovenproof casserole and flatten the top.

Beat the eggs with the milk and add the almonds and raisins. Pour this mixture over the lamb and return the dish, uncovered, to the oven for a further 30 minutes or until the top is lightly browned and puffed.

Serve with plenty of light and crunchy salad.

PER SERVING	
Calories	627.17
Protein g	63.87
Fat g	30.1
Saturated fatty acids g	10.89
Monounsaturated fatty acids g	14.21
Polyunsaturated fatty acids g	4.17
Carbohydrate g	27.66
Total Sugars g	18.3
Sodium mg	311.24
Fiber g	3.22

Legumes are particularly good with relatively fatty meats such as lamb or pork as they absorb the fat thus making it more digestible.

Leg of Lamb Casserole with Beans and Spinach

Serves 8

Because the garlic is cooked long and slowly with the lamb, its flavor is quite mild. Indeed, the whole cloves have been mistaken for cannellini beans !

10	large cloves garlic, peeled but left whole
4 lb 8oz	lean leg of lamb
4 tbsp	olive oil
14 oz	fresh spinach, washed and lightly dried or frozen spinach, defrosted and well drained
1	can (14 oz) green beans, drained
1	can (14 oz) cannellini beans, drained
2	large sprigs fresh rosemary or 2 teaspoons dried
	handful of green peppercorns

Insert 6 garlic cloves into the lamb, then put the rest into a heavy casserole dish (one that you can use on the range) with the oil and the spinach. Cook briskly for 4–5 minutes or until the spinach is wilted. Add the beans, rosemary and green peppercorns.

Lay the leg of lamb on top of the vegetables and beans and cover the casserole tightly. The dish can then be cooked very slowly either on the stove top on in a low oven (300°F) for 3–4 hours.

To serve, remove the lamb from the casserole onto a serving dish and surround with the spinach and bean mixture.

PER SERVING	
Calories	645.8
Protein g	82.64
Fat g	28.81
Saturated fatty acids g	10.96
MonounSaturated fatty acids g	13.39
PolyunSaturated fatty acids g	2.41
Carbohydrate g	14.70
Total Sugars g	1.70
Sodium mg	593.14
Fiber g	6.21

If you have time and think about it in advance you can cook you own legumes, but I find that the small extra expense of buying canned beans is greatly outweighed by their convenience.

Leg of Lamb with Zucchini and Butter Beans

Serves 6

Legumes make particularly good casserole dishes as they absorb the flavors to produce a delicious, and easy to cook, all-in-one meal.

6	cloves of garlic
2 tbsp	olive oil
1 lb 2 oz	zucchini
1 lb 2 oz	canned butter beans, drained
2	large sprigs fresh rosemary
3 lb 5 oz	lean leg of lamb

Peel the garlic cloves and put them, whole, into a heavy oven-proof casserole large enough to hold the lamb. Add the oil, zucchini, butter beans and rosemary. Position the leg of lamb on top of everything.

Cover the casserole tightly and cook very slowly in a very low oven (250°F) for 3 4 hours. Alternatively, you could use a slow cooker. The zucchini and lamb should produce enough moisture not to need any extra liquid but check halfway through the cooking, and if it looks a little dry add 7 oz of water or vegetable stock.

At the end of the cooking time, the lamb should be very tender and the flavors all deliciously amalgamated. It should not need any extra seasoning.

PER SERVING	
Calories	608.17
Protein g	80.39
Fat g	26.10
Saturated fatty acids g	10.62
Monounsaturated fatty acids g	12.70
Polyunsaturated fatty acids g	1.91
Carbohydrate g	13.37
Total Sugars g	2.41
Sodium mg	518.83
Fiber g	4.79

There was a time when you would have needed to salt your eggplant and leave them to drain for some hours to remove their bitterness. However, thanks to modern breeding techniques you can now use them straight from your shopping basket.

Alternative Moussaka

Serves 6

The hummus and Parmesan make a very rich but delicious topping for the moussaka.

2 tbsp	olive oil
2	large eggplants, sliced
10 oz	lean cooked lamb, diced
12 oz	tomatoes, sliced
	salt and pepper
1 hpg tsp	dried marjoram
10 fl oz	yogurt
10 oz	hummus—check ingredients to make sure they do not include wheat starch or gluten
3 oz	grated fresh Parmesan

Fry the eggplant slices in the oil until they are well tanned on each side. Lay half of them out in the bottom of an ovenproof casserole. Lay the lamb over the eggplant and cover it with the sliced tomato. Sprinkle this with salt and pepper and the marjoram. Cover with the remaining eggplant. Mix the yogurt with the hummus and Parmesan and season it lightly, then spoon the mixture over the eggplant. Cook in a moderate oven (350°F) for 20–30 minutes or until the top is well browned. Serve at once.

PER SERVING	
Calories	363.17
Protein g	23.18
Fat g	24.78
Saturated fatty acids g	8.75
MonounSaturated fatty acids g	12.35
PolyunSaturated fatty acids g	2.62
Carbohydrate g	13.03
Total Sugars g	4.8
Sodium mg	453.8
Fiber g	4.30

If your butcher will make you gluten- or wheat-free sausages, make sure that he really understands about contamination. It would be very easy for gluten- or wheat-free sausages to get contaminated by a small amount of breadcrumbs in a busy market, no matter how good his intentions.

Pork Sausages with Oatmeal
(not for celiacs)

Serves 8

If you have a local butcher, he may well be prepared to make you sausages without wheat or gluten.

9 oz	well-trimmed pork fillet or shoulder
2	slices bacon
3 oz	oatmeal, lightly powdered in a food processor
2 oz	onion
1 tsp	salt
½ tsp	black pepper
½ tsp	ground nutmeg
1 tsp	Worcestershire sauce

Put all the ingredients into a food processor or through a mincer so that they are well amalgamated.

Form the mixture into 8 fat or 12 thinner sausages. You can roll them in some extra oatmeal if you wish. Grill or shallow fry for 4–5 minutes and serve with hash brown potatoes or whatever else you would normally serve with sausages.

PER SERVING	
Calories	112.75
Protein g	9.06
Fat g	5.43
Saturated fatty acids g	1.78
Monounsaturated fatty acids g	1.93
Polyunsaturated fatty acids g	.70
Carbohydrate g	7.42
Total Sugars g	0.54
Sodium mg	362.20
Fiber g	0.73

People always assume that sausages have to have skins although skins are really quite unnecessary.

Pork Sausages with Polenta

Serves 8

9 oz	well-trimmed pork fillet / shoulder
1	slice bacon
1	small onion
2 oz	coarse polenta or cornmeal
5 fl oz	water
1 oz	garbanzo (garbanzo/fava bean) flour
1 tsp	salt
½ tsp	black pepper
½ tsp	ground nutmeg
1 tsp	Worcestershire sauce

Process the diced, trimmed pork with the bacon and the onion in a food processor or a mincer. Meanwhile, bring the water to a boil in a small saucepan and add the polenta. Cook gently, stirring continually for several minutes or until the polenta has fully absorbed the water and thickened somewhat. Beat the polenta into the minced pork along with the flour, salt, pepper, nutmeg and Worcester sauce.

Form the mixture into 8 fat sausages. To keep them from being too sticky you can roll them in a little extra flour. Broil or shallow fry for 4–5 minutes or until you are sure they are cooked through, but take care in turning them as the sausages are quite soft and, of course, have no skins so can fall apart quite easily.

Serve with mashed potatoes or whatever else you would normally serve with sausages.

PER SERVING	
Calories	93.72
Protein g	8.64
Fat g	3.74
Saturated fatty acids g	1.30
MonounSaturated fatty acids g	1.39
PolyunSaturated fatty acids g	.64
Carbohydrate g	6.61
Total Sugars g	.520
Sodium mg	314.45
Fiber g	.42

Chicory can be quite bitter if you eat it raw. However, blanching for just a few seconds in boiling water takes the real bitterness out leaving just enough sharpness to counteract the relative blandness of a white sauce.

Ham and Chicory-Stuffed Pancakes

Serves 4

A gluten- and wheat-free version of a classic Belgian dish. The pancakes can be used with any other savory filling.

4 oz	garbanzo (garbanzo/fava bean) flour
	small pinch salt
7 fl oz	water
2 tbsp	sunflower oil
1	medium onion, chopped
1	large head chicory, sliced thickly across the head
1 oz	potato flour
12 fl oz	milk
4 oz	well-flavored ham, sliced into matchsticks
	salt and black pepper
	handful of fresh parsley, chopped

Combine the flour, salt and water in a food processor, and then allow it to stand for 10–15 minutes. Heat a pancake pan with a tiny dribble of oil. Pour one small ladleful of the mixture into the pan and cook quickly on both sides. Each pancake should be quite thin, and you should get four out of the mixture with a couple left over for tasting. Set them aside with plastic wrap or waxed paper between each pancake.

Heat the rest of the sunflower oil in a shallow pan and cook the onion until just beginning to soften. Meanwhile, blanch the chicory in boiling water for 2 minutes only and drain. When the onion is soft, remove from heat and add the potato flour, stirring it well in. Gradually, still off the heat, add the milk and stir until the sauce is quite smooth. Return to the heat and continue to stir until the sauce thickens. Add the ham and chicory and continue to cook for a couple of minutes to allow the flavors to amalgamate. Season lightly to taste with salt and pepper and add the chopped parsley.

Arrange the pancakes either flat on a plate with a layer of the filling in between each to make a "cake," or fill each pancake with

PER SERVING	
Calories	304.20
Protein g	15.08
Fat g	17.29
Saturated fatty acids g	5.29
MonounSaturated fatty acids g	5.46
PolyunSaturated fatty acids g	6.14
Carbohydrate g	24.10
Total Sugars g	6.67
Sodium mg	399.25
Fiber g	3.79

the filling and fold them over. You can arrange them on one big plate or on four individual plates. Cover with plastic wrap and reheat for 2 ½ minutes each for the individual pancakes / about 6 minutes for the cake in a microwave on high. Alternatively, cover tightly with aluminum foil and reheat in a moderate oven for about 30 minutes before serving.

Sweet and Sour Pork

Serves 4

The cornstarch makes a delicious crisp batter for this Chinese flavored pork dish. Excellent with lots of fluffy white rice.

14 oz	pork fillet, trimmed and cubed
1	small egg, beaten
2 oz	cornstarch
	vegetable oil for deep frying
2 tsp	potato flour
4 tbsp	water
4 oz	canned pineapple chunks, with their juice (not syrup)
2½ fl oz	rice or wine vinegar
4 tbsp	sugar (raw cane)
½ tsp	salt
2 tbsp	tomato purée
2 tsp	Worcestershire sauce
2 tbsp	corn oil
1	clove garlic, peeled and finely chopped
1	medium onion, finely chopped
1	medium green bell pepper, deseeded and chopped

Make sure the pork is well trimmed, then toss it in the egg and dredge it in the cornstarch, making sure that every piece is well covered.

Half fill a wok or deep fryer with oil and heat it until a piece of stale wheat- and gluten-free bread browns in 1 minute. Deep fry the pork pieces for approximately 1 minute, making sure that they stay separate, then drain on paper towels.

Meanwhile, dissolve the potato flour in the water and 4 tablespoons of juice from the pineapple. Add the vinegar, sugar, salt, tomato purée and Worcester sauce and mix well.

Heat 1 tablespoon of the corn oil in a clean frying pan, and when it is hot add the garlic and onion, stirring a little; then add the green pepper. Stir-fry for a couple of minutes, season lightly, and add the pineapple chunks. Pour in the sauce and bring to a boil, stirring continuously.

Reheat the deep-frying oil until a piece of bread browns in 50 seconds. Refry the pork pieces for 2–3 minutes to ensure that the outside is crisp without letting the inside dry up. Drain on paper towel and keep warm.

Reheat the sweet and sour sauce and stir in the remaining tablespoon of oil. Pour over the pork and serve at once.

PER SERVING	
Calories	492.07
Protein g	25.23
Fat g	27.12
Saturated fatty acids g	6.06
MonounSaturated fatty acids g	8.26
PolyunSaturated fatty acids g	12.48
Carbohydrate g	41.05
Total Sugars g	27.33
Sodium mg	234.68
Fiber g	1.46

Pork Fillet with Jerusalem Artichokes and Orange

Serves 6

Both pork and lamb fillets are rather under-rated cuts of meat, which is surprising as they are so flexible. Moreover, since there is virtually no wastage, they are a lot more economical than a cut where half of it may turn out to be gristle and fat.

1 lb 10 oz	pork fillet, trimmed of fat and slit open
1 lb	Jerusalem artichokes, scrubbed, trimmed and thinly sliced
4 oz	broken walnuts
2 tbsp	olive oil
2	garlic cloves, crushed
2	medium onions, finely chopped

1	medium cooking apple, peeled and sliced thinly
10 fl oz	dry white wine
10 fl oz	water or homemade chicken or vegetable stock
	freshly squeezed juice of 2 oranges

Open out the pork fillet, sprinkle it lightly with salt and pepper and lay most of the walnuts and half the slices of artichoke down the middle. You should have some walnuts left over; toss these in a little oil and put them aside. You may find it easier to cut the fillet in two completely so as to get the filling well distributed. Tie it into a neat sausage.

Melt the rest of the oil in a heavy casserole and fry the pork roll briskly until it is lightly tanned on each side. Reduce the heat and add the garlic and onion; continue to cook until they soften without turning color, then add the rest of the artichokes, the apples and the liquids. Cover the casserole and simmer it for 50–60 minutes or until the pork is quite tender.

Remove the pork from the casserole, cut the strings and slice the sausage neatly. Lay the slices on a warmed serving dish. Adjust the seasoning to taste and spoon the vegetables and sauce over the pork. Decorate with the remains of the walnuts and serve with brown rice and a green vegetable or salad.

PER SERVING	
Calories	439.25
Protein g	31.98
Fat g	24.91
Saturated fatty acids g	6.26
MonounSaturated fatty acids g	10.19
PolyunSaturated fatty acids g	11.11
Carbohydrate g	16.26
Total Sugars g	8.38
Sodium mg	73.62
Fiber g	4.31

This dish can easily be cooked in advance, then heated in a microwave before serving.

Cauliflower in Cheese Sauce with Bacon and Green Peas

Serves 4

Cauliflower with cheese sauce is so popular as a dish with both adults and children that it is worth working on some variations on that theme. You can use either old or new potatoes for this and fresh or frozen peas.

14 oz	potatoes, scrubbed and cubed
14 oz	cauliflower
7 oz	peas, fresh or frozen
3½ oz	lean bacon slices
1 oz	butter or margarine

1 oz	cornstarch
16 fl oz	low-fat 2% milk
3½ oz	Boursin or other soft, herbed cheese

Scrub the potatoes and quarter them, then steam them for 15 minutes or until they are nearly cooked. Cut the cauliflower into florets and add it to the steamer. Continue to steam for another 5 minutes or until the cauliflower is nearly cooked; then add the peas to the steamer. Continue to steam for a further 3 minutes.

Broil the bacon slices until crisp, remove any excess fat and chop into small pieces.

Meanwhile, melt the butter or margarine and stir in the cornstarch. Gradually add the milk, stirring all the time, over a low heat, until the sauce thickens. Add the herbed cheese and season to taste.

When ready to serve, spoon the vegetables and the bacon pieces into the sauce. Mix gently together, turn into a serving dish and serve at once.

PER SERVING	
Calories	433.44
Protein g	18.96
Fat g	24.81
Saturated fatty acids g	13.84
MonounSaturated fatty acids g	8.77
PolyunSaturated fatty acids g	2.39
Carbohydrate g	35.86
Total Sugars g	9.73
Sodium mg	599.88
Fiber g	5.66

Game birds are relatively expensive as, unlike poultry, they are not intensively bred. Nonetheless, they are worth the occasional splurge, as they do have a flavor you will never get from a domestically raised bird.

Pheasant Braised with White Grapes

Serves 6

This is a very easy way to cook pheasants as it guarantees that they do not dry out while giving them an excellent flavor. Fresh pheasant are usually only available during the winter, but you may find frozen ones year round.

2	large pheasants, trussed
2 oz	butter
12	greens onions, finely chopped
2	sprigs rosemary
16 fl oz	dry white wine
	salt and pepper
8 oz	seedless white grapes, halved

In a heavy casserole, fry the pheasants briskly on all sides in the butter until they are well bronzed all over. Add the onions, reduce the heat and continue to fry more gently until the onions soften. Add the rosemary, wine and a little salt and pepper, cover the casserole and cook gently on the stove top or in a moderate oven (325°F) for 1 hour.

Take out of the oven. Remove the pheasants onto a warmed serving dish, cover and keep warm. Remove the rosemary from the cooking juices, add the grapes and continue to simmer on the stove top for a further couple of minutes to warm the grapes through.

Adjust the seasoning to taste and spoon the grapes and cooking juices around the pheasants. If there is too much to fit, serve the rest in a sauce boat.

Serve with new potatoes or brown rice and a green vegetable or a salad.

PER SERVING	
Calories	566
Protein g	68.2
Fat g	25.26
Saturated fatty acids g	10.65
MonounSaturated fatty acids g	11.37
PolyunSaturated fatty acids g	2.91
Carbohydrate g	6.73
Total Sugars g	6.59
Sodium mg	339.24
Fiber g	.45

Remember that duck, like goose, is a very rich meat so a little goes a very long way.

Duck with Apple and Orange Sauce

Serves 6

A rather less rich version of the classic Duck à l'Orange, and it is given a nice tang by the orange rind.

1	large duck
1	small cooking apple
1	medium onion
1	stick celery
1	tomato
1	sprig parsley
5 fl oz	red wine
10 fl oz	water
	rind and juice of 2 oranges
½ oz	butter
½ oz	potato flour
	salt and pepper

Heat the oven to 350°F.

Prick the duck's skin thoroughly, fill its cavity with the cooking apple, peeled and chopped roughly and roast it for about 1 ½ hours. Meanwhile, make some good stock from the giblets of the duck (reserving the liver) by bringing them to a boil, along with the onion, celery, tomato, parsley, wine, water and a little seasoning, then simmering them for 30–45 minutes.

Meanwhile, carefully peel the rind off the oranges, taking as little pith as possible. Cut it into thin matchsticks and blanch it for a couple of minutes in boiling water.

When the duck is cooked, remove it from the rack and skim as much of the fat off the juices in the roasting tin as you possibly can.

Melt the butter in a saucepan, add the duck liver chopped small and cook for a couple of minutes. Add the potato flour, stir well and cook another minute or two, before adding the juices from the pan, the mushy apple from the cavity of the duck, 10 fl oz of the strained stock and the juice from the 2 oranges. Stir all well together, bring to a boil and simmer for 5–10 minutes.

Meanwhile, carve the duck and lay it on a warmed serving dish, removing as much or as little of the fatty (but crisp) skin as you want. Strain the sauce, return it to the pan, add the orange rinds and reheat. Adjust the seasoning to taste and pour it over the duck. Serve at once with green vegetables and baby new potatoes, if they are available.

PER SERVING	
Calories	225.02
Protein g	25.57
Fat g	8.54
Saturated fatty acids g	3.94
MonounSaturated fatty acids g	4.73
PolyunSaturated fatty acids g	1.25
Carbohydrate g	8.66
Total Sugars g	6.44
Sodium mg	234.25
Fiber g	1.07

Vegetables and Vegetarian Dishes

Baked Potatoes with Tomato and Cheese

Leek, Cucumber and Gruyère Pie

Peanut Butter Bean Pot

Quinoa and Cashew Pilaff

Risotto with Sweet Peppers

Potato, Leek and Apple Pie

Sweet Potato and Tomato Bake

Mushroom and Sunflower Seed Pie

Mexican Rice with Peppers and Corn

Broccoli and Cauliflower au Gratin with Butter Beans

Broccoli and Tofu Stir-Fry

Cranberry and Tofu Risotto

Vegetarian Stuffed Peppers

Slow-Roasted Vegetables with Artichokes

Green Pie for St. Patrick's Day

Beet and Egg Bake

Spinach and Artichoke Pie

Buckwheat Pancakes with Mushroom Sauce

Winter Vegetable Casserole

Carrots Steamed with Butter Beans

Beets with Red Cabbage

Okra and Sweet Potato Bake

Zucchini and Butter Bean Salad

"Dressed" Parsnips

Stir-Fried Brussels Sprouts with Ginger

Pizza Base and Tomato Sauce

Vegetable Dahl

Roman Cabbage

Fava Beans à la Madame

Butter Beans Bourguignon

Baked Polenta with Mushrooms and Cheese

Since children often prefer "baked" potatoes with soft skins while adults like them with crisp skins, starting potatoes in the microwave and then crisping up the skins for those who want them, in the oven, is an excellent way to keep everyone happy.

Baked Potatoes with Tomato and Cheese

Serves 1

A very simple way of "improving" a baked potato—if that is possible!

	1 large or 2 small baking potatoes
1	large tomato, sliced
2 oz	Cheddar cheese, grated
	freshly ground black pepper

Bake the potatoes in the oven or in a microwave until they are cooked through. Take them out of the oven, split them lengthways and open them up. Put them on or in an ovenproof dish. Lay the slices of tomato, layered with the grated cheese, over the open middle of the potato, leaving a layer of cheese on the top. Return the potatoes to a moderately hot oven (350°F) for about 20 minutes to crisp the outside of the skin, cook the tomatoes and melt the cheese. Grind over some black pepper and eat at once.

PER SERVING	
Calories	368.75
Protein g	17.58
Fat g	17.86
Saturated fatty acids g	12.93
MonounSaturated fatty acids g	6.78
PolyunSaturated fatty acids g	1.05
Carbohydrate g	36.78
Total Sugars g	3.58
Sodium mg	356.19
Fiber g	3.35

If you cannot find fresh chilies you can always use dried ones, soaked for 5 minutes in boiling water. Always be careful when dealing with chilies: either wear gloves or wash your hands very well before touching your face or eyes as the chili oil will burn.

Leek, Cucumber and Gruyère Pie

Serves 6

A rather unusual dinner pie, in which the crispness of the water chestnuts sets off the softness of the leeks and pineapple.

7 oz	garbanzo (garbanzo/fava bean) flour, sifted
4 oz	butter or low-fat spread
2 tbsp	sunflower oil
7 oz	leeks, trimmed and sliced
2	fresh red chili peppers, trimmed and sliced
1/2	medium-sized cucumber, diced
4 oz	canned water chestnuts, drained
4 oz	canned pineapple chunks, drained
4 oz	Gruyère or Swiss cheese, sliced
	salt and pepper

Heat the oven to 350°F.

Rub the butter or spread into the flour until it is light and crumbly, then add approximately 4 tablespoons of water to make it into a soft dough. Roll out the pastry and line an 8-inch pie dish. Line it with kitchen foil, weight it down with baking beans and bake the crust alone.

Meanwhile, heat the oil in a flat pan and gently cook the leeks and chili for 5 minutes or until they are beginning to soften. Add the cucumber, cover the pan and gently sauté the vegetables for 10 minutes. Add the drained water chestnuts and pineapple chunks.

Spoon this mixture into the pie dish and lay the slices of cheese over the top.

Bake the pie for 15 minutes just to melt and brown the cheese.

Remove from the oven and grind over some salt and pepper. Serve warm or cold.

PER SERVING	
Calories	363.22
Protein g	11.83
Fat g	26.67
Saturated fatty acids g	13.77
MonounSaturated fatty acids g	6.94
PolyunSaturated fatty acids g	5.17
Carbohydrate g	21.27
Total Sugars g	4.69
Sodium mg	253.08
Fiber g	4.48

If you cannot get fresh ginger-root you can always use 1 teaspoon of ground ginger. The flavor will not be quite the same, but nearly as good. But be sure that it gets well cooked as raw spices do not taste nice.

Peanut Butter Bean Pot

Serves 4

Like all bean pots it pays to make it the day before you want to eat it, to allow the flavors to mature.

8 oz	dried kidney beans
2 tbsp	peanut or sunflower oil
3	sticks celery, diced
2	medium onions, diced
2	medium carrots, sliced into rounds
1	medium red bell pepper, deseeded and sliced
1 oz	gingerroot, peeled and sliced very thinly
½ pint	red wine
1½ pints	water
1 tsp	black peppercorns
3 oz	crunchy peanut butter (check the ingredient list for starch included in some varieties)
	salt
	a good shake of Tabasco
	fresh parsley, chopped roughly

Soak the beans overnight, then discard the water. Alternatively, bring them to a boil in plenty of unsalted water, boil briskly for 10–15 minutes, then drain.

Heat the oil in a heavy pan and gently fry the celery, onion, carrots, pepper and gingerroot for 10–15 minutes or until they have softened slightly.

Add the beans along with the wine, water and peppercorns. Bring the whole lot to a boil and simmer for approximately 1 hour or until the water is absorbed and the beans cooked. If it looks as though the bean pot is getting too dry, add more water. Once the beans are cooked, add the peanut butter, salt (never add it before the beans are cooked or they will go rock hard) and Tabasco to taste. You may find that once the peanut butter is in you need to add a little more water to reduce the sauce. Serve the bean pot generously sprinkled with lots of chopped parsley.

PER SERVING	
Calories	453.99
Protein g	15.83
Fat g	22.21
Saturated fatty acids g	3.08
MonounSaturated fatty acids g	10.77
PolyunSaturated fatty acids g	9.45
Carbohydrate g	38.19
Total Sugars g	9.84
Sodium mg	177.84
Fiber g	13.21

If you cannot find quinoa for this recipe, use an unhusked brown rice.

Quinoa and Cashew Pilaff

Serves 8

Quinoa is a South American gluten-free grain not dissimilar to rice. It has a delicious nutty taste and the crunchy texture of brown rice. You should find it in good delicatessens or health food stores.

4 tbsp	olive oil
10½ oz	leeks, finely sliced
2	sticks celery, chopped
9 oz	quinoa
½ pint	water
½ pint	dry white wine
7 oz	water chestnuts, drained
4 oz	broken cashew nuts
2 oz	sunflower seeds
	juice of 2 fresh lemons
	salt and pepper
2	sprigs fresh mint

Heat the oil in a heavy pan and cook the leeks and celery until just soft. Add the quinoa and the liquid. Bring to a boil and cook gently for 15 minutes until the quinoa is soft and has absorbed the liquid, of which you can add more if necessary. Drain the water chestnuts, halve them and add to the mixture.

Brown the nuts and sunflower seeds in a dry pan and add them to the risotto along with lemon juice, salt and pepper to taste. Just before serving, stir in the fresh chopped mint. Serve warm or cold.

PER SERVING	
Calories	315.13
Protein g	8.87
Fat g	18.66
Saturated fatty acids g	3.03
MonounSaturated fatty acids g	10.44
PolyunSaturated fatty acids g	4.79
Carbohydrate g	24.40
Total Sugars g	4.86
Sodium mg	86.29
Fiber g	1.82

Rices differ enormously in texture and taste. Italian risotto rice is fat, white and soft when cooked, absorbing lots of water. Quite different from a brown unhusked rice which is nutty and crunchy and absorbs relatively little liquid.

Risotto with Sweet Peppers

Serves 4

If you are feeling energetic, char the peppers under a hot broiler, run them under cold water and remove their skins. This does give the peppers an even sweeter and more delicious taste and texture but is time consuming, so can be left out if you are hurried.

4 tbsp	olive oil
2	cloves garlic, sliced
2	large red bell peppers, deseeded and finely sliced
14 oz	canned tomatoes
1	bay leaf
5	fresh basil leaves or 1 teaspoon dried basil
10½ oz	Arborio Italian risotto rice
1½ pints	hot vegetable stock
	salt and pepper

Heat 2 tablespoons of the oil in a large heavy pan. Add the garlic and peppers and cook gently for 5–10 minutes or until the peppers are quite soft. Add the tomatoes, bay leaf and basil.

Continue to cook gently for a further 15 minutes.

Add the rice and mix well. Add half the hot stock, stir well and continue to cook. Stir every now and then to prevent the rice sticking, and when the liquid is absorbed, continue to add more until the rice is quite cooked. Add the rest of the oil and salt and pepper to taste if needed. Leave under cover for 10 minutes before serving.

PER SERVING	
Calories	455.43
Protein g	7.95
Fat g	15.91
Saturated fatty acids g	3.21
MonounSaturated fatty acids g	12.48
Carbohydrate g	69.79
PolyunSaturated fatty acids g	2.89
Total Sugars g	9.69
Sodium mg	237.69
Fiber g	2.40

Use a tart eating apple such as a Granny Smith and add a squeeze of lemon juice.

Potato, Leek and Apple Pie

Serves 6

The apples give a refreshing sharpness to this dish.

3 lb 5oz	potatoes, well scrubbed
4 tbsp	olive oil
3	medium onions, peeled and roughly chopped
4–5	sticks of celery, chopped
2	large tart apples, peeled, cored and diced
2 tbsp	potato flour
16 fl oz	milk
3 oz	hazelnuts
	salt and pepper
	sesame seeds

Slice the potatoes quite thinly and par-cook them in a steamer or microwave. They will take around 10 minutes depending on the type of potato. Lay half of them out in the bottom of a flat, ovenproof dish and reserve the rest.

Meanwhile, heat 3 tablespoons of the oil in a heavy pan and gently cook the onions, celery, apple until the onion and celery are soft but not brown. Add the potato flour, stir around well, then gradually add the milk and continue to cook until the sauce thickens slightly.

Break up the hazelnuts in a food processor until they are approximately halved, and then lightly brown them under a broiler or in a pan with no oil, shaking all the time. Add hazelnuts to the celery mixture. Season to taste.

Spoon this mixture over the potatoes and cover with the remaining slices of potato, layered tightly on top of each other. Brush the top of the potatoes with the remaining tablespoon of oil and sprinkle over the sesame seeds.

Bake the dish in a moderate oven (350°F) for 20–30 minutes or until the dish is well heated through and the potatoes on top are lightly browned. Serve at once.

PER SERVING	
Calories	570.78
Protein g	12.71
Fat g	30.38
Saturated fatty acids g	9.53
MonounSaturated fatty acids g	23.49
PolyunSaturated fatty acids g	4.59
Carbohydrate g	65.77
Total Sugars g	15.54
Sodium mg	388.10
Fiber g	7.48

Sweet potatoes or yams are increasingly popular and are now to be found in most supermarkets.

Sweet Potato and Tomato Bake

Serves 6

This combination of vegetables is quite sweet, although really delicious, so serve it with a crisp green salad with a tart lemon dressing to redress the balance.

2 lb 4oz	sweet potato, peeled and sliced thinly
3 tbsp	sunflower oil
2 lb 4oz	tomatoes, sliced
1 oz	sugar (raw cane)
7 oz	Cheddar cheese, grated
10 fl oz	fresh heavy cream or—if you wish to lower the fat content—crème fraîche
	salt and pepper
2	small packs plain potato chips, crushed with a rolling pin

Heat two tablespoons of the oil in a heavy pan and briskly fry the sweet potato slices on both sides until they are tanned. Meanwhile, grease a casserole dish with the rest of the oil. Layer the sweet potato slices and the tomatoes alternately, sprinkling each layer lightly with salt, pepper, sugar, cheese and cream and ending with a layer of sweet potato topped with cream and cheese. Sprinkle the crisps over the top and bake in a moderately hot oven (325°F) for 40–50 minutes or until the sweet potato is cooked and the top well tanned.

PER SERVING	
Calories	642.03
Protein g	13.07
Fat g	44.6
Saturated fatty acids g	23.93
MonounSaturated fatty acids g	13.94
Polyunsaturated fatty acids	5.66
Carbohydrate g	50.51
Total Sugars g	20.46
Sodium mg	477.79
Fiber g	6.08

When using frozen spinach, always remember to drain it very thoroughly, pressing the water out with the back of a wooden spoon. It retains a great deal of water which can spoil a dish like this flan.

Mushroom and Sunflower Seed Pie

Serves 4

A lovely filled pastry for a summer lunch, it can be prepared in advance and tastes as good cold as warm.

3 oz	garbanzo (garbanzo/fava bean) flour
3 oz	rice flour
3 oz	butter or low-fat spread
3 tbsp	walnut or sunflower oil
5 oz	fresh baby corns, whole or halved as you prefer
2 oz	sunflower seeds
7 oz	button mushrooms, rinsed and dried, whole if they are small, otherwise halved
3 oz	fresh spinach or defrosted frozen leaf spinach
	juice of 1 lemon
	salt and freshly ground black pepper

Heat the oven to 350°F.

Make the pastry by rubbing the butter or spread into the flour then adding enough water to make a firm dough. Roll it out and line an 8–9-inch pie dish. Prick the bottom, line it with foil and weight it with beans or rice. Bake it for 10 minutes with the foil in, then 10 minutes without to get it nice and crisp.

Meanwhile, heat the oil in a heavy pan and add the corn and sunflower seeds. Fry briskly until they are lightly tanned all over. Add the mushrooms, reduce the heat slightly and continue to cook for a couple of minutes. Then add the chopped spinach, stir well, cover the pan and cook for a further couple of minutes. Remove the lid, add the lemon juice and season well. Make sure the ingredients are well amalgamated before spooning them into the pie shell. Serve at once warm, or cool and serve at room temperature.

PER SERVING	
Calories	460.50
Protein g	10.04
Fat g	34.37
Saturated fatty acids g	12.02
MonounSaturated fatty acids g	7.67
PolyunSaturated fatty acids g	13.13
Carbohydrate g	28.58
Total Sugars g	2.22
Sodium mg	394.86
Fiber g	4.84

Canned peppers are a useful standby to keep in the cupboard. They do not have the crunch of fresh peppers but are very flavorsome and colorful if you are using them in a cooked dish.

Mexican Rice with Peppers and Corn

Serves 6

This is a really pretty dish, with the peppers and corn contrasting delightfully with the white rice.

3 tbsp	sunflower oil
2	medium onions, peeled and finely chopped
1	small green bell pepper, deseeded and finely sliced
1	small red bell pepper, deseeded and finely sliced
1	small yellow bell pepper, deseeded and finely sliced
1	red chili pepper, deseeded and finely sliced
10 oz	white basmati rice
1 pint	homemade vegetable stock or water
4 oz	canned sweetcorn niblets, drained
5 fl oz	plain yogurt
2 oz	Cheddar cheese, grated
	salt
	Tabasco

Heat the oil in a heavy pan and gently cook the onions, peppers and chili until they are beginning to soften.

Add the rice, stir for a minute or two, then gradually add the stock. Bring to a boil and cook briskly until the liquid is absorbed and the rice is cooked. If necessary, add a little more stock.

Add the sweetcorn, yogurt and cheese and stir in well. Season to taste with the salt and, if you want it to taste hotter, add Tabasco. Serve just warm or at room temperature.

If the dish is too dry, add a little more vegetable stock.

PER SERVING	
Calories	338.58
Protein g	8.84
Fat g	11.42
Saturated fatty acids g	3.44
MonounSaturated fatty acids g	3.33
PolyunSaturated fatty acids g	5.39
Carbohydrate g	50.17
Total Sugars g	7.01
Sodium mg	114.91
Fiber g	1.65

Polenta with Gorgonzola
(page 22)

French Toast with Bacon
(page 28)

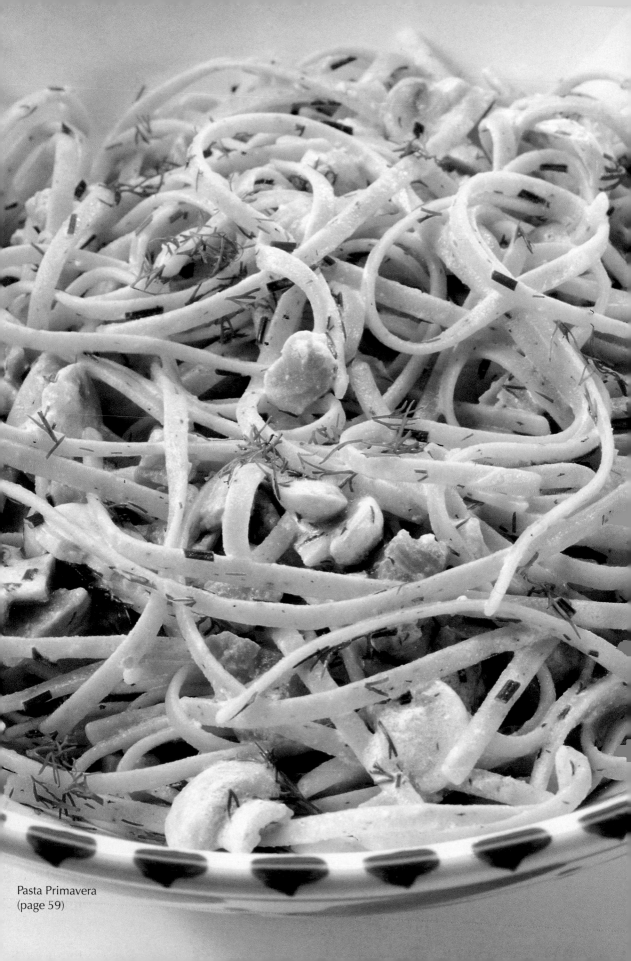

Pasta Primavera
(page 59)

Pizza Base and Tomato Sauce
(page 136)

Pancakes
(page 147)

Carrot and Ginger Tart
(page 144)

Fruit Crumbles
(page 160)

Cheese Scones
(page 167)

Top—Lemon Shortcakes
(page 172);
Bottom—Aunt Vi's Ginger Cookies
(page 182)

Light Sponge Cake
(page 183)

Yorkshire Pudding
(page 188)

Top—Wholemeal Loaf
(page 191);
Middle—Golden Yeast Loaf
(page 194);
Bottom—Rice and Corn Soda Bread
(page 190)

If you cannot get fresh cauliflower or broccoli for any dish, you can use frozen but add them only at the end of the cooking process and make sure not to do more than heat them through or they will become very soggy.

Broccoli and Cauliflower au Gratin with Butter Beans

Serves 6

Cauliflower and cheese is always a popular dish so it seems worth using it as a basis for other variations on the same theme.

1	large onion, peeled and chopped
10 oz	cauliflower florets
1 lb 2 oz	broccoli florets
2 oz	butter
2 oz	potato flour
1 tbsp	wholegrain mustard
1 pint	milk
5 oz	Cheddar cheese, grated
2 tbsp	fresh Parmesan, grated
1	can (15 oz) butter beans, drained
1 oz	flaked almonds
1	small pack ordinary potato chips, crushed
	salt and pepper

Steam or microwave the onion, cauliflower and broccoli florets until they are just cooked but still slightly *al dente*. Set aside.

Meanwhile, melt the butter in a large pan and add the potato flour to make a roux. Add the mustard, then gradually add the milk, stirring continuously until you get a smooth sauce. Add two-thirds of the cheeses and stir until they are melted. Season to taste, remembering that the chips on the top will probably already be salted.

Carefully add the vegetables, the butter beans and the almonds and, mixing gently, gradually bring the dish back to just below boiling point.

To serve, spoon the mixture into a heat-proof casserole dish, mix the remaining cheese with the potato chips, sprinkle them over the top of the dish and pass under the broiler to brown lightly.

PER SERVING	
Calories	425.22
Protein g	22.58
Fat g	27.18
Saturated fatty acids g	14.86
MonounSaturated fatty acids g	8.73
PolyunSaturated fatty acids g	2.60
Carbohydrate g	24.11
Total Sugars g	9.85
Sodium mg	632.98
Fiber g	6.44

If you do not have a wok you can still stir fry quite successfully in a deep, large frying pan. Just make sure that your oil is very hot and that you work quickly.

You can buy ready marinated tofu in most health food stores although you should check its ingredients. If you cannot get it, use a normal tofu but marinate in 1 tablespoon of mushroom ketchup and 1 tablespoon of lemon juice for an hour before using it.

Broccoli and Tofu Stir-Fry

Serves 4

Broccoli is always wonderful in a stir-fry as it keeps its color so well. Do not be tempted to season with soy sauce unless you are sure it is a wheat- and gluten-free brand.

4 tbsp	sunflower or stir-fry oil
1 oz	fresh gingerroot, peeled and very finely sliced
2	large cloves garlic, finely sliced
1	small green chili, deseeded and very finely sliced
4 oz	Jerusalem artichokes, well scrubbed and finely sliced in rounds
14 oz	broccoli, the stem sliced thinly and the heads broken into small florets
7 oz	marinated tofu, cubed
2 oz	sesame seeds
	mushroom ketchup

Heat the oil in a wok and briskly fry the ginger, garlic and chili. Do not allow them to burn.

Add the broccoli stems and finely sliced artichoke to the vegetables in the wok and continue to cook for a further few minutes.

Add the broccoli florets, tofu and sesame seeds and continue to cook briskly for a further 3–4 minutes or until the florets are just beginning to soften.

Serve at once seasoned with mushroom ketchup to taste.

PER SERVING	
Calories	295.50
Protein g	11.72
Fat g	25.32
Saturated fatty acids g	3.55
MonounSaturated fatty acids g	6.58
PolyunSaturated fatty acids g	14.45
Carbohydrate g	5.93
Total Sugars g	2.29
Sodium mg	42.74
Fiber g	4.62

Most people only think of using cranberries at Christmas but they are a delicious, tart fruit to use at any time of the year, and you can always use frozen berries if you can't get fresh ones.

Cranberry and Tofu Risotto

Serves 4

A brightly colored risotto. The cranberries and red bell pepper contrast strikingly with the rice while the crunch of the water chestnuts contrasts equally well with the softness of the tofu.

2 tbsp	olive oil
2	medium leeks, finely sliced
1	medium-sized red pepper, deseeded and finely sliced
5 oz	risotto rice
4 oz	fresh cranberries
1	large, tart eating apple, peeled, cored and diced
½ pint	dry white wine
1 pint	water
9 oz	smoked or marinated tofu, diced
7 oz	canned water chestnuts, drained and halved
	salt and pepper

Heat the oil in a heavy pan then gently cook the leeks and peppers until soft.

Add the rice, cranberries and apple, then the wine and water, stirring gently. Bring to a simmer and cook gently for 10–15 minutes or until the rice is soft and the liquid absorbed. Add a little more liquid if necessary.

Add the tofu and the water chestnuts. Mix well and season to taste with salt and pepper. Serve warm or cold.

PER SERVING	
Calories	352.05
Protein g	9.65
Fat g	11.21
Saturated fatty acids g	2.06
MonounSaturated fatty acids g	7.10
PolyunSaturated fatty acids g	2.90
Carbohydrate g	42.79
Total Sugars g	10.61
Sodium mg	208.94
Fiber g	2.74

You can always make the stuffing for any stuffed pepper dish in advance and freeze it, merely defrosting it at room temperature for a couple of hours before you use it.

Vegetarian Stuffed Peppers

Serves 6

A good dish for a buffet as they can be cooked in advance and are easy to eat with a fork—or even fingers!

2 tbsp	olive oil
1	large onion, roughly chopped
3	large cloves garlic, peeled and finely chopped
3	fresh red chilies, deseeded and finely chopped
1	large red bell pepper, sliced
9 oz	green lentils
1¾ pints	water
	salt and freshly ground black pepper
2 oz	pitted black olives
1 tbsp	sunflower seeds
3	large yellow bell peppers, halved and with the seeds and ribs removed
	large bunch fresh parsley

Heat the oil in a large pan and cook the onion, garlic, chilies and red bell pepper until they are all softening and lightly tanned but not burned. Add the lentils, stir for a couple of minutes, then add the water. Bring to a boil and simmer for 20–30 minutes or until the lentils are cooked without being totally mushy. You may need to add more liquid as they cook. Add the olives and sunflower seeds, mix them well in, then season to taste with salt and pepper.

Pile the mixture into the yellow pepper shells—if you have too much pile it round the outside of the shells—and, depending on how crisp you like your pepper shells, put them in a moderately hot oven (375°F), covered, for 10–30 minutes. Sprinkle them lavishly with the chopped parsley just before serving. The peppers are good either hot or cold.

PER SERVING	
Calories	250.28
Protein g	12.97
Fat g	9.68
Saturated fatty acids g	2.4
MonounSaturated fatty acids g	6.22
PolyunSaturated fatty acids g	2.76
Carbohydrate g	29.93
Total Sugars g	8.97
Sodium mg	237.68
Fiber g	6.93

You can roast almost any combination of vegetables this way. A very easy and nutritious way to cook them.

Slow-Roasted Vegetables with Artichokes

Serves 4

A splendidly easy and quite delicious way to cook vegetables to be eaten on their own or as an accompaniment to roast meat.

4 tbsp	olive oil
4	turnips, peeled and sliced
4	leeks, sliced
1	medium red bell pepper, seeded and sliced
4 oz	fresh spinach or frozen spinach leaf, defrosted
2	cans (15 oz) artichoke hearts, drained
2	cans (15 oz) fava beans, drained
2 tbsp	pumpkin seeds
1 tbsp	mushroom ketchup or tomato ketchup
	black pepper

Preheat the oven to 350°F.

Put the oil in the bottom of an ovenproof casserole and add all the other ingredients except the pumpkin seeds and mushroom ketchup. Cover the casserole and cook in the oven for 30–40 minutes or until the turnips are soft. If you are in a hurry, cook the vegetables in a microwave on high for 4 minutes then transfer to the oven for 20 minutes. Add the pumpkin seeds, mushroom ketchup and black pepper to taste.

Serve alone or with rice, baked potatoes or bread.

PER SERVING	
Calories	404.95
Protein g	20.81
Fat g	25.03
Saturated fatty acids g	6.01
MonounSaturated fatty acids g	16.24
PolyunSaturated fatty acids g	8.03
Carbohydrate g	26.86
Total Sugars g	10.78
Sodium mg	31.85
Fiber g	17.52

You could serve the pie with homemade wheat- and gluten-free bread colored green with lots of fresh herbs !

Green Pie for St. Patrick's Day

Serves 6

This is a lovely quiche for any day of the year but particularly good on March 17th when anyone with a speck of Irish blood wears green.

7 oz	sifted garbanzo (garbanzo/fava bean) flour
3½ oz	butter
1	large, ripe avocado
2 oz	pumpkin seeds
1 oz	shelled pistachio nuts
4 oz	fresh spinach
1 tsp	fresh marjoram or ½ tsp dried
4	medium eggs
16 fl oz	milk
	salt
	black pepper

Heat the oven to 325°F.

Rub the butter into the flour until you have a sandy consistency. Add enough water to make a stiff paste and roll out. Line an 8-inch pie dish with the pastry, prick with a fork then line it with foil and weight it with beans or rice to bake it empty: 10 minutes with the foil, then 10 minutes with the foil and beans or rice removed.

Peel and pit the avocado and chop its flesh into reasonably sized dice. Put the flesh in a large bowl with the pumpkin seeds and the pistachio nuts. Chop the spinach and add it along with the marjoram. In a separate bowl beat the eggs, add the milk and season well. Add the liquid mixture to the green mixture, mix them well and spoon into the pie shell.

Bake in the oven for 35 minutes or until it is set and slightly risen. Serve warm or cold.

PER SERVING	
Calories	457.21
Protein g	17.75
Fat g	33.52
Saturated fatty acids g	14.08
MonounSaturated fatty acids g	11.34
PolyunSaturated fatty acids g	4.78
Carbohydrate g	23.08
Total Sugars g	5.75
Sodium mg	283.63
Fiber g	5.41

Beet and Egg Bake

Serves 4

A must for beet enthusiasts as it brings out not only the wonderful color but the flavor of fresh beets.

10 oz	beets, topped and tailed,scrubbed and diced
10 oz	turnips, topped and tailed, scrubbed and diced
10 oz	tart eating apples, cored but not peeled, diced
	sea salt or table salt
	fresh ground black pepper
4	large eggs
1 tbsp	sesame seeds

Put the beets, turnips and apples in a large steamer and steam for approximately 20 minutes or until all are cooked. Purée in a food processor and season to taste with a little salt and pepper.

Spoon the mixture into a flat ovenproof dish, smooth out and make 4 hollows. Break the eggs into the hollows and sprinkle over the sesame seeds.

Bake in a moderate oven (325°F) for 15 minutes or until the eggs are just set—they should not wobble when you shake the dish—and the topping is lightly tanned. Serve at once.

PER SERVING	
Calories	200.58
Protein g	10.84
Fat g	10.49
Saturated fatty acids g	4.63
PolyunSaturated fatty acids g	3.29
MonounSaturated fatty acids g	6.43
Carbohydrate g	17.76
Total Sugars g	17.13
Sodium mg	341.86
Fiber g	4.84

It is worth keeping a stock of fresh seeds—pumpkin and sunflower in particular—in the cupboard as they make excellent snacks for wheat and gluten allergics and can be carried in a bag in your pocket or handbag.

Spinach and Artichoke Pie

Serves 6

Another excellent dish that can be prepared in advance and eaten warm or at room temperature.

4 oz	garbanzo (garbanzo/fava bean) flour
2 oz	butter
5 oz	cottage cheese
5 oz	frozen leaf spinach, defrosted and drained
2 oz	pumpkin seeds
5 oz	artichoke hearts, canned or frozen and drained or defrosted
2 oz	Gruyère cheese
	pepper

Heat the oven to 350°F.

Rub the butter into the flour until you have a sandy consistency. Mix with a little water to make a soft dough. Roll out the pastry, line a 6-inch pie dish and bake empty (see Green Pie recipe, preceding).

Spread the cottage cheese over the bottom of the pie shell.

Mix the spinach with the pumpkin seeds and spread it over the cottage cheese.

Arrange the artichoke hearts on the top, then sprinkle liberally with the grated Gruyère. Return to the oven for a further 20 minutes.

Grind over some fresh black pepper as the pie comes out of the oven and serve hot or warm.

PER SERVING	
Calories	214.37
Protein g	8.82
Fat g	15.47
Saturated fatty acids g	7.79
MonounSaturated fatty acids g	4.12
PolyunSaturated fatty acids g	2.67
Carbohydrate g	10.82
Total Sugars g	1.61
Sodium mg	78.23
Fiber g	2.75

You might want to make a double batch of the pancake mixture as they are equally good with any other savory filling and freeze well for future use.

Buckwheat Pancakes with Mushroom Sauce

Serves 4

Because the buckwheat flour is dark, both the pancakes and the mushroom filling are quite a dark, rich color so serve them with a light, bright vegetable such as snow peas or a green salad with lots of yellow peppers.

3½ oz	buckwheat flour
1	large egg
3½ fl oz	water
5 fl oz	milk
2 tbsp	olive oil
1	medium onion, peeled and finely chopped
1	clove garlic, finely chopped
7 oz	button mushrooms, rinsed, dried and sliced
1 oz	potato flour
10 fl oz	milk
2 oz	broken cashew nuts
1 oz	halved black olives
	salt and pepper
	fresh parsley, chopped

To make the pancakes:

Process the buckwheat flour, egg, pinch of salt, water and milk in a food processor and allow batter to stand for 10–15 minutes.

Heat a pancake pan with a tiny dribble of oil. Pour one-eighth of the mixture into the pan and cook quickly on both sides. The pancakes should be quite thin and you should get eight out of the mixture. Set them aside with a layer of plastic wrap or waxed paper between each pancake.

To make the stuffing:

Heat the olive oil in shallow pan and cook the onion and garlic until just beginning to soften. Add the mushrooms and continue to cook briskly until the mushrooms are done and their juices running.

Remove from the heat and add the potato flour. Stir it well in, then gradually add the milk and stir until the sauce is quite smooth.

PER SERVING	
Calories	375.81
Protein g	12.27
Fat g	21.32
Saturated fatty acids g	5.90
MonounSaturated fatty acids g	11.94
PolyunSaturated fatty acids g	2.55
Carbohydrate g	36.40
Total Sugars g	8.14
Sodium mg	528.10
Fiber g	2.73

Return to the heat and continue to stir until the sauce thickens. Add the cashews and the olives and continue to cook for a couple of minutes to allow the flavors to amalgamate. Season lightly to taste with salt and pepper and add the chopped parsley.

Arrange the pancakes either flat on a plate with a layer of filling between each to make a "cake," or fill each pancake separately and fold them over. You can arrange them on one big plate or on four individual plates. Cover with plastic wrap and reheat for 2½ minutes each for the individual pancakes / about 6 minutes for the cake in a microwave on high. Alternatively, cover tightly with aluminium foil and reheat in a moderate oven for about 30 minutes before serving.

Like the oven-baked vegetables, this is another dish where you can vary the vegetables according to what you have in your fridge, or your own personal favorites.

Winter Vegetable Casserole

Serves 8

A very easy dish to prepare and excellent either on its own or as an accompaniment to roast meat or a vegetarian roast.

10½ oz	potatoes
10½ oz	parsnip
10½ oz	rutabaga
10½ oz	celeriac
7 oz	celery
7 oz	fennel
6	bay leaves
1 lb 12 oz	canned tomatoes
3½ fl oz	dry white wine
10½ oz	Brussels sprouts
	large handful of fresh parsley

Peel and cut the root vegetables into fairly large dice or pieces. Chop the fennel and celery. Put both lots of vegetables into a heavy, ovenproof casserole with the bay leaves, tomatoes and white wine. Mix together well, cover and cook gently in a low oven (300°F) for up to an hour or until all the vegetables are almost cooked. Stir every now and then to mix the vegetables.

When the root vegetables are all but cooked, add the sprouts and continue to cook for 15 minutes until the sprouts are soft but not soggy.

Adjust the seasoning although salt or pepper should not be needed.

Just before serving, sprinkle large quantities of freshly chopped parsley over the vegetables.

PER SERVING	
Calories	117.71
Protein g	4.79
Fat g	1.81
Saturated fatty acids g	1.55
MonounSaturated fatty acids g	1.59
PolyunSaturated fatty acids g	.94
Carbohydrate g	19.74
Total Sugars g	10.01
Sodium mg	77.83
Fiber g	8.04

Use young but not miniature vegetables for maximum flavor.

Carrots Steamed with Butter Beans

Serves 6

If you want to turn this into a meat dish—very popular with children—add 7 ½ oz frankfurters, sliced in thick rounds, along with the butter beans and peas; omit the lemon juice and oil.

1 lb 5oz	young carrots, sliced in moderately thick rounds
2	cans (14 oz) butter beans, drained
14 oz	frozen green peas
4 fl oz	fresh lemon juice
6 tbsp	olive oil
	salt and black pepper

Steam the carrots in a large steamer for 15–20 minutes or until they are just cooked. Add the butter beans and peas and continue to steam for a further 5 minutes until all are well warmed through.

Remove from the steamer into a dish and dress with the salt, pepper, lemon juice and olive oil—you may need to adjust the seasoning to your own taste.

PER SERVING	
Calories	306.72
Protein g	12.52
Fat g	16.99
Saturated fatty acids g	2.67
PolyunSaturated fatty acids g	2.79
MonounSaturated fatty acids g	13.12
Carbohydrate g	28.19
Total Sugars g	9.46
Sodium mg	662.65
Fiber g	11.86

A combination of Brussels sprouts and red cabbage, finely sliced, also makes an excellent winter salad, especially when mixed with cooked potato.

Beets with Red Cabbage

Serves 4

A wonderfully colored dish with a very Russian feel to it.

7 oz	small raw beets, scrubbed and halved or quartered if large
9 oz	Brussels sprouts, trimmed and halved if large
7 oz	red cabbage, sliced
1 oz	currants
1 tsp	caraway seeds
3 tbsp	red wine
3 tbsp	water
3 tbsp	plain low-fat yogurt
2 oz	broken cashew nuts
1 oz	sesame seeds
1/2 tsp	potato flour
5 fl oz	milk
9 fl oz	plain low-fat yogurt
	juice of 1/2–1 lemon
	salt and pepper

Steam the beets in a steamer for 5 minutes, then add the sprouts. Continue to cook for a further 10–15 minutes or until both are *al dente*. Cut the beets into medium-sized dice.

Meanwhile, put the red cabbage, currants and caraway seeds in a large, heavy pan with the wine, water and yogurt. Cover and cook gently for 10–15 minutes or until the cabbage is also *al dente*.

Mix all the vegetables together, then add the cashews and sesame seeds. You can stop at this point and serve the dish warm on its own or as a vegetable.

If you want to make the sauce, mix the potato flour with a little of the milk to make a smooth paste. Add the rest of the milk and heat slowly, stirring all the time, until the sauce thickens. Remove from the heat and add the yogurt and lemon juice, then season to taste. Reheat but do NOT boil or the sauce will curdle, and pour over the vegetables to serve.

PER SERVING	
Calories	264.41
Protein g	12.63
Fat g	13.07
Saturated fatty acids g	4.25
MonounSaturated fatty acids g	6.63
PolyunSaturated fatty acids g	4.19
Carbohydrate g	24.24
Total Sugars g	19.57
Sodium mg	324.37
Fiber g	5.93

Brightly colored dishes like this are great to serve in winter as they make you feel as though there is sun around, even when there is not !

Okra and Sweet Potato Bake

Serves 4

Another brightly colored vegetable casserole that works just as well as a dish on its own or as an accompaniment to any well flavored meat dish.

2	large green chilies, deseeded and finely sliced
1	large clove garlic, finely sliced
5 ½ oz	okra, topped and tailed and sliced into rings
7 oz	fresh or frozen leaf spinach
14 oz	canned tomatoes
3 ½ fl oz	vegetable stock
5 ½ oz	green beans, topped and tailed and sliced across
	salt and pepper
1 lb 5oz	sweet potato, peeled and very thinly sliced
1 tbsp	olive oil

Heat the oven to 350°F.

Put the chili, garlic, okra, spinach and tomatoes in a heavy pan and bring gently to a boil. Simmer for 15–20 minutes, adding a little vegetable stock if the mixture seems too dry. Add the green beans and season to taste. Spoon the mixture into an ovenproof casserole.

Lay the sweet potatoes out over the top, carefully overlapping each slice. Cover the casserole and cook in a moderate oven for 25 minutes or until the sweet potatoes are almost cooked.

Remove the lid, brush the top of the potatoes with the oil, and return to the oven, uncovered, for a further 15 minutes to brown the top.

PER SERVING	
Calories	278.56
Protein g	9.63
Fat g	9.62
Saturated fatty acids g	1.88
MonounSaturated fatty acids g	5.59
PolyunSaturated fatty acids g	2.01
Carbohydrate g	41.23
Total Sugars g	14.71
Sodium mg	4567.46
Fiber g	7.90

As always, if you do not like cilantro, substitute it with flat leaved or ordinary fresh parsley.

Zucchini and Butter Bean Salad

Serves 6

A substantial salad to serve as a main course or, in smaller quantities, as a starter.

6 tbsp	olive oil
6	medium zucchini, thickly sliced
10 oz	marinated or smoked tofu, in fairly large dice
1 lb	canned butter beans, drained
4 oz	pitted black olives
	salt and pepper
	fresh cilantro, roughly chopped

Cook the zucchini briskly in the oil until they are all lightly tanned but still *al dente*. Add the tofu, butter beans and olives (whole or halved as you prefer) and cook on a very low heat for 5 minutes to allow the flavors to amalgamate. Remove from the heat and season to taste with salt and pepper.

The salad can be served warm or at room temperature but in either case stir in the fresh, chopped cilantro just before serving.

PER SERVING	
Calories	262.6
Protein g	10.45
Fat g	19.67
Saturated fatty acids g	2.79
MonounSaturated fatty acids g	13.39
PolyunSaturated fatty acids g	3.21
Carbohydrate g	11.89
Total Sugars g	2.66
Sodium mg	759.67
Fiber g	4.68

If you are a sweet potato fan, you could also try this recipe with sweet potatoes.

"Dressed" Parsnips

Serves 6

This is a seventeenth-century recipe and is quite the most delicious way of serving parsnips that I know.

2 lb 4 oz	parsnips, scrubbed and sliced
1¾ pints	milk

Put the parsnips in a large saucepan with the milk and bring gently to a boil. Simmer for 45 minutes–1 hour or until the parsnips are quite soft. Drain them, reserving the milk. Purée them in a food processor or liquidizer, then return them to the pan. Reheat them slowly, gradually stirring in all the milk that they were cooked in. You can add seasoning if you want, but I did not find it was necessary. Serve them at once or set aside and reheat to serve when needed.

PER SERVING	
Calories	216.67
Protein g	8.33
Fat g	8.33
Saturated fatty acids g	4.33
MonounSaturated fatty acids g	2.67
PolyunSaturated fatty acids g	.50
Carbohydrate g	28.83
Total Sugars g	17.50
Sodium mg	108.33
Fiber g	7.67

If you want to keep the Chinese feel and make your family really work for their supper, get them to eat the sprouts with chopsticks!

Stir-Fried Brussels Sprouts with Ginger

Serves 4

Most people think of Brussels sprouts only as a rather overcooked green vegetable with Christmas turkey but they have endless other possibilities as vegetables. Do not be tempted to use soy sauce unless you are absolutely sure that it does not contain wheat or gluten.

2 tbsp	sesame, stir-fry or sunflower oil
4	large cloves of garlic, peeled and very thinly sliced
1½ oz	fresh gingerroot, peeled and very finely sliced
14 oz	Brussels sprouts, trimmed and finely sliced
3 oz	broken cashew nuts
	salt and pepper

Heat the oil in a wok and lightly fry the garlic and ginger for 4–5 minutes, making sure they do not burn. Add the sprouts and cashew nuts and cook quite fast for 2–3 minutes or until the sprouts are just beginning to soften. Season with salt and pepper and serve at once.

PER SERVING	
Calories	225.01
Protein g	7.48
Fat g	18.01
Saturated fatty acids g	3.17
MonounSaturated fatty acids g	8.17
PolyunSaturated fatty acids g	5.67
Carbohydrate g	9.13
Total Sugars g	4.28
Sodium mg	81.66
Fiber g	4.91

The simplest pizza topping is a tomato sauce, but you can add variety with additional toppings such as:
• grated cheese
• slices of Mozzarella
• olives
• capers
• sliced mushrooms
• diced peppers
• salami
• bacon
• ham
• sweetcorn

Pizza Base and Tomato Sauce

Serves 4

Pizza is such a popular dish these days, especially with kids, that it is important to have a recipe for it. This recipe make a slightly "bready" but very acceptable pizza base.

5 oz	garbanzo (garbanzo/fava bean) flour
½ tsp	salt
¼ tsp	instant yeast granules
scant tbsp	olive oil
about 6 tbsp	lukewarm water
14 oz	canned tomatoes
1	large clove garlic, chopped
½ tsp	dried basil
	pinch dried oregano
	pinch dried parsley
	salt
	pepper

Mix the flour, salt and yeast granules in a bowl. Make a well in the middle and add the oil; then, gradually, stirring all the time with a fork, add the warm water. Continue to mix until you have a rough ball of dough. (If it is too sticky, add more flour; if there are dry patches of flour, add more water.) Once the dough has come together in a ball, take it out and knead it by pushing it flat with the ball of your hand, then folding it over into a new ball and flattening it all over again. You should continue to knead for 8–10 minutes, by which time the dough should have become quite elastic.

Put the ball of dough into a clean bowl, cut a cross in the top with a knife, cover the bowl tightly with plastic and put it in a warm, draft free place to rise. It should roughly double its size in 1–3 hours depending on the room temperature.

When the dough has risen, take it out of the bowl and "knock" the air out of it with your fist. On a floured board, knead it again for a further few minutes, then flatten it with your hands. Roll the dough out with a rolling pin until it is no more than 1 inch thick in the middle and a little thicker at the edge. Place it on a flat baking sheet.

Spread with tomato sauce (see below) and your chosen topping, then bake in a hot oven (400°F) for 8–12 minutes or until the topping and base are cooked. Serve at once.

PER PIZZA	
Calories	470.00
Protein g	22.00
Fat g	4.00
Saturated fatty acids g	0.40
MonounSaturated fatty acids g	0.90
PolyunSaturated fatty acids g	1.90
Carbohydrate g	85.00
Total Sugars g	33.00
Sodium mg	210.00
Fiber g	18.00

Tomato pizza topping
Put the tomatoes and garlic in a pan over low heat and cook gently for 30 minutes. Add the herbs and continue to cook for a further 30 minutes until the tomatoes are well reduced. Season to taste.

Real Indian dahls are often quite liquid and are used more as a sauce than a dish on their own. The garam masala may be found in health food or Indian stores.

Vegetable Dahl

Serves 4

Dahl always seems to bring out the best in lentils. This makes an excellent quick supper dish.

2 tbsp	sunflower oil
2	medium onions, finely sliced
1	large clove garlic, finely chopped
½ tsp	ground cumin
¼ tsp	cayenne pepper
14 oz	eggplant, diced
4 oz	red lentils
1 pint	water or homemade vegetable stock
	salt
1 tsp	tomato purée
8 oz	potatoes, scrubbed and diced
8 oz	cauliflower florets
1 tsp	ground turmeric
2 tsp	garam masala

PER SERVING	
Calories	251.28
Protein g	11.4
Fat g	9.21
Saturated fatty acids g	2.3
MonounSaturated fatty acids g	3.81
PolyunSaturated fatty acids g	5.51
Carbohydrate g	33.13
Total Sugars g	7.81
Sodium mg	83.78
Fiber g	5.91

Heat the oil in a heavy pan and gently fry the onions, garlic, cumin and cayenne for a couple of minutes. Add the eggplant, lentils, stock, salt and tomato purée, cover and simmer for approximately 30 minutes.

Meanwhile, put the potatoes and cauliflower in two separate pans with a bare 1 inch of water in the bottom of each to which you have added ½ teaspoon of turmeric. Cover them both and simmer until the vegetables are just tender, then drain.

When the eggplant mixture is ready, stir in the garam masala to taste and the drained vegetables. Serve with rice and, if possible, Indian bread.

Not only did the Romans believe that cabbage would cure hangovers but that lettuce would send you to sleep !

Roman Cabbage

Serves 4

This recipe is based on a Roman recipe that used cracked wheat instead of rice.

4 oz	brown rice
½ oz	butter
1	medium onion, finely sliced
450 g	savoy cabbage, chopped
5 fl oz	homemade vegetable stock or water
	salt and pepper
2 oz	pine nuts
2 oz	raisins
10	coriander seeds
1 oz	butter

Cook the rice in plenty of fast-boiling water or vegetable stock until it is just *al dente*.

Meanwhile, cook the finely sliced onion gently in the butter until it is transparent. Add the cabbage, mix the onion well in and then add the stock and a little seasoning. Cover the pan and simmer gently for approximately 15 minutes or until the cabbage is cooked but still slightly crunchy; it can also be cooked in a microwave for approximately 5 minutes on high.

Turn the cabbage into an ovenproof dish. Stir the pine nuts, raisins and coriander seeds into the rice and season lightly if needed. Spread the mixture over the cabbage and dot the top with butter. Cover and cook in a moderate oven (350°F) for 20 minutes to allow the flavors to amalgamate before serving.

PER SERVING	
Calories	322.33
Protein g	6.45
Fat g	18.12
Saturated fatty acids g	6.51
MounounSaturated fatty acids g	6.02
PolyunSaturated fatty acids g	6.01
Carbohydrate g	35.95
Total Sugars g	15.25
Sodium mg	138.53
Fiber g	4.80

If you cannot get fava beans, you can still use the same recipe with other dried beans; the taste will not be as authentic but it will still be good.

Fava Beans, à la Madame

Serves 6

Slowly cooked brown fava beans or *ful* is the national dish of Egypt. The beans are eaten by rich and poor, for breakfast, lunch and dinner, with bread, lentils, sauces, salads and slow-cooked eggs. Seasoning, apart from the addition of some garlic once the beans are cooked, is done at the table.

1 lb 10 oz	dried brown fava beans
4	large cloves garlic, finely chopped
	large bunch of fresh parsley

Soak the rinsed beans for a minimum of 8 hours. Then put them in a large saucepan well covered with fresh water, bring to a boil, cover and simmer until they are tender but not mushy. This can take anywhere from 2–6 hours depending on how dry the beans were; if you have a slow cooker it can be used to cook the beans overnight. You can also cook them in a pressure cooker, which reduces the cooking time to 30–45 minutes. Remember that a microwave will not reduce the cooking time. When the beans are cooked, drain them and add the garlic.

Serve the beans warm, in bowls sprinkled with chopped parsley. Accompany them with oil or butter and lemon juice, salt, pepper, cumin and cayenne pepper.

PER SERVING	
Calories	368.6
Protein g	24.39
Fat g	2.25
Saturated fatty acids g	.50
MonounSaturated fatty acids g	.16
PolyunSaturated fatty acids g	1.01
Carbohydrate g	66.89
Total Sugars g	4.75
Sodium mg	52.88
Fiber g	20.55

If you cannot get button onions, use pickling onions or, if they drive you mad to peel, just use the smallest onions you can find and halve them.

Butter Beans Bourguignon

Serves 6

An excellent vegetarian version of Boeuf Bourguignon.

2 tbsp	sunflower oil
2	cloves garlic, crushed
9 oz	button onions, peeled but left whole
2	small sticks celery, chopped
1	small red bell pepper, deseeded and sliced
7 oz	button mushrooms, rinsed, dried and left whole
1 tsp	dried thyme
	small bunch fresh parsley, chopped
2	bay leaves, fresh or dried
10	black peppercorns
1 oz	potato flour
10 fl oz	red wine
10 fl oz	homemade vegetable stock or water
14 oz	butter beans, canned and drained
14 oz	green beans, canned and drained
14 oz	cannellini beans, canned and drained

Heat the oil in a heavy pan and gently cook the garlic, onions, celery and pepper until soft but not brown.

Add the mushrooms, herbs and peppercorns. Continue to cook for another few minutes, then add the potato flour. Make sure it is well amalgamated before adding the red wine and the stock; season lightly. Bring back to a boil and simmer gently for 30 minutes.

Add all 3 cans of beans and gradually bring back to a boil and simmer until the beans are well heated through. Adjust seasoning to taste before serving.

PER SERVING	
Calories	317.39
Protein g	16.94
Fat g	6.72
Saturated fatty acids g	1.51
MonounSaturated fatty acids g	4.68
PolyunSaturated fatty acids g	3.9
Carbohydrate g	41.67
Total Sugars g	6.63
Sodium mg	1070.77
Fiber g	13.27

Baked Polenta with Mushrooms and Cheese

Serves 6

A favorite north Italian dish. This recipe is based on one in Anna del Conte's wonderful book, *The Classic Food of Northern Italy*. You can make the polenta the day before you need it, then combine it with the sauce when you need to cook the dish.

7 oz	coarse polenta
1 ¾ pints	water
3 tbsp	olive oil
3	whole cloves garlic, peeled but left whole
14 oz	mixed mushrooms of your choice, roughly chopped
6	leaves fresh basil, chopped
1 oz	butter
1 oz	cornstarch
10 fl oz	whole milk
4 fl oz	medium sherry
4 oz	Mozzarella
7 oz	Gorgonzola
4 oz	Parmesan
	sea salt

Heat the oven to 350°F.

Bring the water to a simmer with the salt in a medium saucepan. Gradually add the polenta to the water (Italians would let it run through their fingers) stirring all the time. Bring back to the simmer and cook, stirring all the time, for 5 minutes. Oil a shallow ovenproof dish and spoon in the polenta mix. Cover with oiled foil and bake for 1 hour.

Take out of the oven and, with the foil still on top, allow the polenta to get quite cold.

To make the bake, reheat the oven.

Heat the oil in a heavy pan and add the garlic cloves, mushrooms and basil. Cook briskly for 5–8 minutes or until the mushrooms are cooked through.

PER SERVING	
Calories	540.22
Protein g	23.57
Fat g	34.41
Saturated fatty acids g	17.07
PolyunSaturated fatty acids g	1.97
MonounSaturated fatty acids g	12.56
Carbohydrate g	31.33
Total Sugars g	3.92
Sodium mg	970.15
Fiber g	.84

Meanwhile, melt the butter in a small pan, add the cornstarch, mix well, and then gradually add the milk, stirring all the time until the sauce thickens. Add the sherry.

Use a couple of tablespoons of the sauce to cover the bottom of a large ovenproof casserole.

Turn the polenta out onto a board and cut half of it into medium-thick (¼ inch) slices and arrange a layer over the sauce. Spoon the mushrooms over the polenta, then cover it with slices of the Mozzarella and Gorgonzola. Cut the remains of the polenta into more slices with which to cover the cheese.

Finally, cover the top layer of polenta with the rest of the sauce and sprinkle over the grated Parmesan.

Return to the oven and bake for a further 30 minutes to melt and amalgamate the cheese and sauces. Serve at once with a green salad.

Desserts

Carrot and Ginger Tart

Tipsy Cake

Cheesecake Pancakes

Pancakes

Hot Chocolate Soufflé

Fresh Fruit Sponge Cake

Chocolate Roulade

Apple and Vermicelli Pudding

Crêpes Suzettes

Trifle

Bakewell Tart

Lemon Meringue Pie

Bread and Butter Pudding

Steamed Marmalade Pudding

Cranberry Rice Pudding

Lemon Cheesecake

Fruit Crumbles

Rhubarb Crumble (not for celiacs)

Baked Fruit Tart

*Oat and Raspberry Crumble
(not for celiacs)*

Sweet Rum Omelette

Upside Down Ginger and Pear Cake

Natural fruit sweeteners like puréed carrots, apples or pears give a delicious flavorsome sweetness, quite unlike—and much nicer than—the cloying sweetness of white sugar.

Carrot and Ginger Tart

Serves 4

A rather unusual, but delicious, tart which uses the natural sweetness of carrots to contrast with the spiciness of the ginger.

2 oz	sieved garbanzo (garbanzo/fava bean) flour
2 oz	rice flour
3 oz	butter
2 oz	broken walnuts
10 oz	young carrots, scrubbed and sliced thickly
1 hpg tsp	ginger powder
4 tbsp	sweet white dessert wine
4 tbsp	apple juice
2	eggs
2 oz	crystallized (candied) or stem ginger rinsed free of syrup/sugar

Mix the flours together and rub in the butter. When it is well crumbled, add the walnuts and enough water to make a firm paste. Roll this out and line a 7-inch pie dish; reserve the pastry scraps. Line the crust with foil, weight it with beans and bake it in a moderate oven (350°F) for 10 minutes. Remove the beans and foil and cook for a further 5 minutes or until the pastry is cooked through; then take it out of the oven and set it aside.

Meanwhile, put the carrots in a heavy pan with the ginger, wine and apple juice, cover it tightly and simmer it gently for 30 minutes by which time the carrots should be quite soft. Purée the carrots in a food processor with the 2 eggs.

Chop the crystallized ginger into quite small pieces (how small will depend on what size bits you would like to find in your tart) and mix them into the carrot purée. Spoon this into the crust and use the pastry scraps to decorate the top with lattice work ribbons, pastry balls or decorate with finely grated carrot. Reduce the oven to 325°F and return the tart for 20 minutes, by which time the pastry decoration should be cooked and the filling set. Serve warm or cold with cream, yogurt or ice cream.

PER SERVING	
Calories	400.21
Protein g	9.69
Fat g	28.36
Saturated fatty acids g	12.07
MonounSaturated fatty acids g	7.72
PolyunSaturated fatty acids g	7.38
Carbohydrate g	24.88
Total Sugars g	8.01
Sodium mg	222.5
Fiber g	3.98

If you are making this for children to eat, substitute their favorite fruit juice for the sherry and brandy.

Tipsy Cake

Serves 10

This is a great dessert for a party as it looks so spectacular yet is very easy to make and can be prepared well in advance. If you prefer a lighter sponge use the rice flour sponge cake on page 183

7 oz	butter
7 oz	sugar (raw cane)
3	medium eggs
7 oz	sifted garbanzo (garbanzo/fava bean) flour
1 hpg tsp	wheat- and gluten-free baking powder
1 tsp	vanilla extract
10 fl oz	medium sweet sherry
4 tbsp	brandy
2 oz	flaked almonds
1 pint	frozen yogurt or lightly whipped cream

Beat the butter with the sugar until light and fluffy. Beating slowly, add the eggs alternately with the flour. Fold in any remaining flour, baking powder and vanilla. Spoon into a well-oiled or lined 8-inch cake pan and bake in a moderate oven (350°F) for 30 minutes or until the cake is firm to the touch and a toothpick comes out clean. Cool on a rack.

Arrange your cake on a serving dish and prick it thoroughly all over with a skewer.

Mix the brandy with the sherry or wine and slowly pour it over the cake allowing it to soak in thoroughly; your cake should end up really soggy.

Stick the almonds all over the cake. Serve it accompanied by the frozen yogurt or whipped cream.

PER SERVING	
Calories	459.47
Protein g	10.89
Fat g	25.76
Saturated fatty acids g	13.55
MonounSaturated fatty acids g	8.01
PolyunSaturated fatty acids g	2.23
Carbohydrate g	38.76
Total Sugars g	29.11
Sodium mg	276.36
Fiber g	2.51

Cheesecake Pancakes

Serves 4

You can use these pancakes with any other sweet mixture that you fancy.

4 oz	garbanzo (garbanzo/fava bean) flour
7 fl oz	water
12 oz	plain cream cheese or cottage cheese
3 oz	plump raisins
	juice of 1 lemon
1½ oz	superfine sugar
	salt

Mix the flour, salt and water in a food processor, then allow it to stand for 10–15 minutes. Heat a pancake pan with a tiny dribble of oil. Pour one small ladleful (⅛) of the mixture into the pan and cook quickly on both sides; stack them with a piece of plastic wrap between each pancake.

In a bowl, mix the cheese with the raisins, lemon juice and sugar to taste. Divide the mixture in 8 and fill each pancake; fold each pancake into a neat parcel and place in an ovenproof serving dish. Sprinkle them with the extra sugar and put them under a hot broiler to caramelize the sugar topping. Serve at once.

PER SERVING	
Calories	268.58
Protein g	11.41
Fat g	7.79
Saturated fatty acids g	4.13
MonounSaturated fatty acids g	2.26
PolyunSaturated fatty acids g	1.00
Carbohydrate g	41.12
Total Sugars g	29.37
Sodium mg	145.9
Fiber g	3.07

Do involve children when you are making pancakes. Whether or not they actually make them, they can still have great fun tossing them—and if you lose a few to the floor, the mixture is so cheap that it really does not matter.

Pancakes

Serves 4

These pancakes freeze well so it might be worth making a big batch and freezing them, interleaved with plastic wrap or waxed paper so that you can just peel off as many as you need.

4 oz	garbanzo (garbanzo/fava bean) flour
	salt
7 fl oz	water
1 tbsp	sunflower oil
	juice of 2 lemons
¼ cup	superfine sugar

Mix the flour, salt and water in a food processor, then allow it to stand for 10–15 minutes. Heat a pancake pan with a tiny dribble of oil. Pour one small ladleful of the mixture into the pan and cook quickly on both sides.

The pancakes should be quite thick and you should get at least 8 out of the mixture.

If they are to be eaten at once, serve them from the pan with sugar and lemon juice.

If they are to be used for a later dish, stack them with a piece of plastic wrap between each pancake.

PER SERVING	
Calories	163.31
Protein g	5.18
Fat g	5.40
Saturated fatty acids g	.88
MonounSaturated fatty acids g	1.34
PolyunSaturated fatty acids g	3.35
Carbohydrate g	26.01
Total Sugars g	14.26
Sodium mg	107.84
Fiber g	2.71

Soufflés are a great deal easier to make than everyone reckons—and very impressive. As long as you fold in plenty of well-whisked (but not overwhipped) egg white you should be fine.

Hot Chocolate Soufflé

Serves 4

Although this is light it is seriously rich, so serve it after a light meal—and have plenty of coffee ready !

5	egg whites
	small pinch salt
7 oz	superfine sugar
2 oz	cocoa powder
	few drops vanilla extract

Heat the oven to 350°F and put in a bain marie (a baking pan containing water) big enough to hold the soufflé dish. Allow the water to get warm. Lightly grease the soufflé dish.

Whisk the egg whites with the salt until pretty stiff. Whisk in 3 tablespoons of the sugar, then fold in the rest with the cocoa powder and the vanilla. Spoon the mixture into the soufflé dish and cook in the bain marie for 30–40 minutes or until the soufflé is risen and crisp on top.

Serve at once with low-fat milk, cream or yogurt.

PER SERVING	
Calories	254
Protein g	7.31
Fat g	3.21
Saturated fatty acids g	2.10
MonounSaturated fatty acids g	1.40
PolyunSaturated fatty acids g	.58
Carbohydrate g	54.44
Total Sugars g	53.13
Sodium mg	240.53
Fiber g	1.51

If you want to be economical about this cake, use slightly bruised fruit and put lots of it in the middle of the cake with plenty of cream cheese.
Then just sprinkle the top with powdered sugar.

Fresh Fruit Sponge Cake

Serves 10

This is a very flexible dessert that can be made with any fresh or canned fruit of your choice.

1	light sponge cake
7 oz	plain cream cheese
10 fl oz	whipping cream
10 oz	strawberries or other fresh seasonal fruit

Make the sponge cake according to the recipe on page 184.

When it is cold, cut it in half horizontally and spread the lower half with the cheese.

Put a thin layer of fruit, sliced or halved if necessary, over the cheese and cover with the top of the cake.

Whisk the cream until is holds its shape and use it to cover the cake. Top the cream with the fresh fruit arranged in whatever pattern you choose.

PER SERVING	
Calories	420.39
Protein g	12.26
Fat g	20.87
Saturated fatty acids g	11.53
MonounSaturated fatty acids g	7.38
PolyunSaturated fatty acids g	1.60
Carbohydrate g	47.70
Total Sugars g	30.23
Sodium mg	104.74
Englyst Fiber g	1.04

If you are using this for a party, you can make it one, or even two days ahead, but only sprinkle it with powdered sugar when you are ready to use it.

Chocolate Roulade

Serves 8

A real 1960s favorite that has stood the test of time—and which has the advantage of containing no wheat or gluten !

6 oz	dark chocolate
5	eggs
6 oz	superfine sugar
3 tbsp	hot water
1 oz	powdered sugar
½ pint	heavy cream

Preheat the oven to 350°F.

Line a 12-inch jellyroll pan with waxed paper and brush it well with oil.

Break the chocolate into a double boiler and melt it slowly. Meanwhile, separate the eggs and whisk the yolks with the sugar until it is lemon colored. Remove the chocolate from the heat, stir in the hot water, then mix the chocolate with the egg yolk mixture. Whisk the whites until they hold their shape and fold them into the chocolate mixture. Pour all into the 12-inch jellyroll pan, make sure it is evenly spread and bake it for 15 minutes or until it holds its shape when lightly pressed with a finger. Make sure the oven shelf is level or you will get a lopsided roll.

Once the roulade is cooked, take it out of the oven, cover it with a clean sheet of waxed paper topped with a wet tea towel and leave it for at least a couple of hours.

To finish the roulade, turn it onto a third piece of waxed paper, well dusted with powdered sugar. Carefully peel off the waxed paper. Whisk the cream until it holds its shape, spread it over the roulade, then carefully roll it up, removing the lower sheet of waxed paper, and turn it onto a serving dish. Shake a little more powdered sugar over the top. You can eat it immediately but it will be very squishy; chill it for a couple of hours to firm it up.

PER SERVING	
Calories	436.81
Protein g	6.60
Fat g	28.44
Saturated fatty acids g	16.11
MounounSaturated fatty acids g	9.01
PolyunSaturated fatty acids g	1.24
Carbohydrate g	41.81
Total Sugars g	40.62
Sodium mg	70.25
Fiber g	0.00

When dealing with rice noodles, you need to cook them in fast-boiling water so as to keep them moving and separated; otherwise they have a habit of getting stuck together in a lump.

Apple and Vermicelli Pudding

Serves 4

This recipe is based on a popular Victorian apple dessert.

2	large cooking apples
2 tsp	ground cinnamon
1 oz	sugar (raw cane)
	juice of ½ lemon
7 fl oz	water
2 oz	raisins
2 oz	rice noodles
2	eggs, separated

Heat the oven to 350°F.

Core the apples, chop them and put them in a saucepan with the cinnamon, sugar, lemon juice and water. Bring to a boil and simmer for 5–8 minutes or until the apples are cooked. Purée them (complete with skins) in a food processor and add the raisins.

Meanwhile, cook the noodles in plenty of fast boiling water for 4 minutes. Drain them and mix in the raisins and the apple mixture. Separate the eggs and stir the yolks into the apple and noodle mixture. Lightly whisk the egg whites and fold them into the mixture.

Turn the pudding into an oiled deep pie dish and bake for 30 minutes, by which time the pudding should be lightly risen, set and lightly browned on top. Serve warm, by itself or with cream or yogurt.

PER SERVING	
Calories	195.38
Protein g	5.16
Fat g	3.61
Saturated fatty acids g	2.89
MonounSaturated fatty acids g	3.37
PolyunSaturated fatty acids g	0.63
Carbohydrate g	37.61
Total Sugars g	27.43
Sodium mg	50.15
Fiber g	2.32

You can make all the elements of the crêpes in advance and freeze them individually, ready for final reheating and assembly when you are ready.

Crêpes Suzettes

Serves 6

A classic dish that works well with wheat- and gluten-free pancakes.

5 oz	garbanzo (garbanzo/fava bean) flour
	salt
9 fl oz	water
4	lumps of sugar
	rind and juice of 2 oranges
3 oz	superfine sugar
7 oz	butter
7 fl oz	Cointreau or Grand Marnier
6 tbsp	brandy

For the pancake mixture, mix the flour, salt and water in a food processor and then allow it to stand for 10–15 minutes.

Rub the sugar lumps over the oranges until the sides of the lumps have absorbed all the oil from the orange skins. Remove the peel of the oranges with a vegetable peeler or very sharp knife, making sure that you do not get any pith.

Mash the sugar lumps on a chopping board with the point of a heavy knife, then add the orange peel and the superfine sugar and chop them all together until they are very finely minced. Scrape the mixture into a mixing bowl. Add the softened butter and beat with an electric mixer if possible until the mixture is light and fluffy. Drop by drop add the orange juice and 2 oz of the orange liqueur—it must be done slowly or the butter will not absorb the liquid.

Heat a pancake pan with a tiny dribble of oil. Pour one small ladleful of the pancake mixture into the pan and cook quickly on both sides. Stack the pancakes as you make them with a piece of plastic wrap between each pancake; you should get at least 12 out of the mixture.

To serve:

Put the butter mixture in a reasonably large chafing dish or heavy frying pan and heat slowly until it is bubbling. Dip both sides of each crêpe in the butter until it is warm, fold it in half and then in half again to make a wedge and stack the crêpes at the side of the pan. Pour over the remaining orange liqueur and stir into the sauce.

Warm the brandy in a ladle or pan then pour it gently over the crêpes and light immediately, before it has time to amalgamate with the rest of the sauce. If you are nervous that it will not catch, cheat by lighting the brandy while it is still in the ladle and pour it over as it is flaming. Serve the crêpes at once.

PER SERVING	
Calories	552.22
Protein g	6.48
Fat g	28.65
Saturated fatty acids g	18.79
MonounSaturated fatty acids g	7.54
PolyunSaturated fatty acids g	2.21
Carbohydrate g	44.18
Total Sugars g	32.43
Sodium mg	330.82
Fiber g	3.81

If this is for children, substitute their favorite fruit juices for the brandy and sherry.

Trifle

Serves 8

The garbanzo flour makes quite a solid sponge, which I think works well with trifle. If you prefer a lighter mixture, use the rice flour sponge on page 183.

4 oz	butter
4 oz	sugar (raw cane)
1	large egg
4 oz	sifted garbanzo (garbanzo/fava bean) flour
1 hpg tsp	wheat- and gluten-free baking powder
2	egg yolks
³⁄₄ oz	potato flour
2 tbsp	superfine sugar
½ tsp	vanilla extract
10 fl oz	milk
3 tbsp	brandy
3½ fl oz	sweet sherry
7 oz	canned peaches, drained
3½ fl oz	whipping cream
½ tsp	superfine sugar
1 tsp	browned flaked almonds

Sponge:

Beat the butter with the sugar until light and fluffy. Beating slowly, add the egg with some of the flour. Fold in the remaining flour and baking powder. Spoon into a well-oiled or lined 6-inch baking pan (the shape does not matter) and bake in a moderate oven (350°F) for 20 minutes or until the cake is firm to the touch and a toothpick comes out clean. Cool on a rack.

Custard:

In a small saucepan, mix the egg yolks with the potato flour, sugar and vanilla, and then gradually add the milk. Heat slowly, stirring all the time, until the custard thickens. Cool.

PER SERVING	
Calories	357.80
Protein g	6.81
Fat g	15.95
Saturated fatty acids g	9.02
MonounSaturated fatty acids g	5.11
PolyunSaturated fatty acids g	1.68
Carbohydrate g	44.50
Total Sugars g	36.63
Sodium mg	190.67
Fiber g	2.00

Do not tell anyone that you have made a dish with wheat- and gluten-free ingredients. The chances are that no one will notice, so your allergic family member will not be made to feel the odd one out, yet again.

PER SERVING	
Calories	445.64
Protein g	11.2
Fat g	29.07
Saturated fatty acids g	8.17
MonounSaturated fatty acids g	13.5
PolyunSaturated fatty acids g	5.55
Carbohydrate g	37.24
Total Sugars g	20.68
Sodium mg	187.38
Fiber g	3.44

Trifle:

Break up the sponge cake in the bottom of a glass or china bowl and pour over the brandy and sherry. The cake should be really well soaked.

Cover the cake with the drained fruit, cut the peaches in half if they are too big, then spoon the egg custard over the fruit.

Whisk the whipping cream with the sugar until it just holds its shape and spoon it over the custard. Sprinkle with almonds over the top, cover with plastic wrap and refrigerate until needed.

Bakewell Tart

Serves 8

Classic dishes are often barred to wheat and gluten allergics, but both this and the recipe for Lemon Meringue Pie on page 155 show that you can create excellent alternatives that everyone will be happy to eat.

4 oz	sifted garbanzo (garbanzo/fava bean) flour
4 oz	rice flour
6 oz	butter
5 oz	superfine sugar
7 oz	ground almonds
1/2 tsp	almond extract
2	eggs

Heat the oven to 350°F.

Rub half the butter into the mixed flours until they are light and crumbly, then add approximately 4 tablespoons water to make a soft dough. Roll out the pastry and line an 8-inch pie dish saving any trimmings to decorate the dish. Line it with kitchen foil, weight it down with baking beans and bake it for 10 minutes. Remove the foil and beans and return to the oven for a further 10 minutes.

For the filling, beat the remaining butter, sugar, ground almonds, almond extract and eggs together in a bowl. Spoon the filling into the tart shell and decorate the top with the remaining pastry rolled out and cut into strips for lattice work. Bake for 30 minutes, and if the top looks as though it is burning turn the oven down slightly.

Serve warm or cold, alone or with cream, plain yogurt or ice cream.

I think that using raw cane sugar in the lemon curd gives it a better flavor, but you do lose the lemony color—so you must make the choice!

Lemon Meringue Pie

Serves 6

4 oz	sifted garbanzo (garbanzo/fava bean) flour
4 oz	rice flour
4 oz	butter or margarine
1 ⅛ cups	superfine sugar
1 ½ oz	potato flour
6 fl oz	water
2	eggs, separated
2 oz	butter
	grated rind and juice of 2 large lemons

Heat the oven to 350°F.

Rub the butter into the flours until the mixture is light and crumbly, then add approximately 4 tablespoons of water to make it into a soft dough. Roll out the pastry and line an 8-inch pie dish with kitchen foil, weight it down with baking beans and bake it for 10 minutes. Remove the foil and beans and return to the oven for a further 10 minutes.

Meanwhile, mix ¾ cup of the sugar thoroughly with the potato flour in a pan, add the water and bring it to a boil over a low heat, stirring constantly. Cook until it thickens and remove it from the heat. When it has cooled slightly, add the egg yolks and stir vigorously. Return to a very low heat and gradually add the butter in little bits and the lemon juice and rind. Taste to make sure that it is not too tart (or too sweet) and add more sugar or lemon accordingly. Spoon the filling into the pastry shell.

Beat the two egg whites until they are stiff. Then add the remaining sugar and continue to whisk until the meringue is very stiff and shiny. Spoon over the top of the filling, making sure that it is totally covered. Bake in a hot oven (375°F) for 8–10 minutes or until the top of the meringue is lightly tanned. Remove and cool before eating.

PER SERVING	
Calories	500.92
Protein g	7.68
Fat g	23.88
Saturated fatty acids g	14.42
MonounSaturated fatty acids g	6.34
PolyunSaturated fatty acids g	1.57
Carbohydrate g	69.64
Total Sugars g	43.59
Sodium mg	238.02
Fiber g	2.52

Do not tell anyone that you have made a wheat- and gluten-free Bread and Butter Pudding. The custard will disguise the rather different texture of the bread so it will be fun to see if anyone notices.

Bread and Butter Pudding

Serves 6

Another great favorite usually barred to celiacs and wheat intolerants—but now gloriously resurrected !

4	slices of wheat- and gluten-free bread
1 oz	butter
1 oz	currants
1 oz	raisins
	the rind of 1 lemon, cut off thinly with a sharp knife
1 oz	sugar (raw cane)
1	whole egg
1	egg yolk
1 oz	superfine sugar
14 fl oz	milk

Butter a pie dish, then butter the bread. Cut the slices of bread in four. Put a layer of bread in the bottom of the dish, cover it with half the fruits, lemon peel and 1 oz sugar. Cover this with another layer of bread, another layer of fruits, etc., and the final layer of bread.

Beat the egg with the egg yolk, most of the superfine sugar and the milk. Pour this carefully down the side of the dish (not over the top of the bread) and leave to soak for a couple of hours.

To cook, sprinkle the last of the sugar over the top of the pudding and bake it in a moderately cool oven (325°F) for 30–45 minutes or until the custard is set and the top is brown and crispy. Serve warm.

PER SERVING	
Calories	227.75
Protein g	7.33
Fat g	9.32
Saturated fatty acids g	4.73
MonounSaturated fatty acids g	2.81
PolyunSaturated fatty acids g	0.67
Carbohydrate g	30.87
Total Sugars g	17.10
Sodium mg	267.98
Fiber g	1.33

You can vary the texture of the pudding quite dramatically by varying the marmalade—from a darkish one with lots of peel, which I like, to a very pale one with very thin slivers of peel.

Steamed Marmalade Pudding

Serves 6

You can also steam the pudding in a microwave for 8–10 minutes on high, although I never think microwaved puddings are quite as light.

4 oz	margarine
2 oz	sugar (raw cane)
2	eggs
4 oz	sifted garbanzo (garbanzo/fava bean) flour
1 hpg tsp	wheat- and gluten-free baking powder
5 ½ oz	dark marmalade with large chunks of peel
7 oz	creamy yogurt
	juice of 1 lemon
	juice of 1 orange

Beat the margarine with the sugar. Beat in the eggs, accompanying each with a tablespoon of flour. Fold in the rest of the flour with the baking powder and the marmalade. Spoon the mixture into a well-greased bowl (it should come about ⅔ of the way up) and cover it tightly with waxed paper held in place with string or a rubber band.

Put the bowl in a large saucepan so that the pudding has room to rise. Carefully pour water round the bowl until it comes about half way up. Cover the pan, bring back to a boil and simmer up to 2 hours.

For the sauce, carefully mix the fruit juices into the yogurt.

To serve, turn the pudding onto a warmed serving plate and pour the sauce over.

PER SERVING	
Calories	287.33
Protein g	9.07
Fat g	13.12
Saturated fatty acids g	4.57
MonounSaturated fatty acids g	5.22
PolyunSaturated fatty acids g	2.77
Carbohydrate g	36.73
Total Sugars g	28.72
Sodium mg	233.02
Fiber g	1.96

Fresh cranberries are very high in vitamin C.

Cranberry Rice Pudding

Serves 4

An interesting variation on a standard rice pud. If you do not like coconut milk you can use regular cow's milk, but in that case you will need to sweeten it with 1–2 teaspoons of sugar. The coconut milk is naturally very sweet so no extra sugar is needed.

2 oz	short-grained rice
1 oz	cranberries
½ pint	coconut or sweetened cow's milk
	1 vanilla pod or 3 drops vanilla extract

If you are using the vanilla pod put it in the milk and bring it just to a boil, then allow to cool.

Put the rice, cranberries and milk (discarding the vanilla pod if used or with the vanilla extract if you are not using a pod) into an ovenproof dish. Mix around and put in a low oven (300°F) uncovered. Cook very slowly for 2 ½–3 hours, stirring whenever you happen to remember.

Serve warm or cold, alone or with cream, yogurt or ice cream.

PER SERVING	
Calories	62.50
Protein g	1.18
Fat g	0.30
Saturated fatty acids g	0.23
MonounSaturated fatty acids g	0.83
PolyunSaturated fatty acids g	0.83
Carbohydrate g	13.91
Total Sugars g	4.06
Sodium mg	82.65
Fiber g	0.98

If you prefer a crumbly base to the cheesecake, you could use the recipe for lemon shortbread or ginger cookies. Crumble them, then mix them with 4 tablespoons of melted butter. Press this mixture into the bottom of the pan to make the base.

Lemon Cheesecake

Serves 6

A delicious treat without cooking!

½	rice flour sponge cake (see page 183) cut in half horizontally
⅓ oz	gelatin
	grated rind and juice of 2 lemons
8 oz	cottage cheese
3 oz	superfine sugar
7 fl oz	whipping cream
2 oz	raisins

Lay half the sponge cake out on the bottom of a removable-bottom cake pan.

Soak the gelatin in the lemon juice, heat it until the gelatin dissolves then cool. Mix the lemon rind, cottage cheese, sugar, cream, and gelatin well together. Fold in the raisins. Spoon the mixture over the sponge cake and chill for at least four hours. Unmold, with the cake on the bottom, and transfer onto a serving dish.

PER SERVING	
Calories	472.85
Protein g	11.57
Fat g	30.52
Saturated fatty acids g	17.99
MonounSaturated fatty acids g	8.94
PolyunSaturated fatty acids g	1.70
Carbohydrate g	42.19
Total Sugars g	36.11
Sodium mg	198.79
Fiber g	1.55

Fruit Crumbles

Serves 6

Fruit crumbles can be made with any combination or variety of fruits that you fancy. In each case they need to be gently stewed with a little water and a sweetener of your choice (sugar, honey, fruit concentrate, etc.). Drain off any extra juice before you put them into the pie dish and reserve it to be served with the crumble. If there is too much juice, it will make the topping soggy.

   Toppings can also be widely varied. You can use nuts or seeds as we have in the recipe below. Alternatively, you may want a more conventional crumble topping—or you may not want to eat oats. In that case mix together:

2 oz	butter or margarine
3 oz	sifted garbanzo (garbanzo/fava bean) flour
2 oz	rice flour
3 oz	superfine sugar

Rub the butter into the flours. Mix in the sugar. Once the mixture is really sandy, spread it over the fruit in the pie dish and bake in a moderate oven for 30 minutes to crisp the top.

Rhubarb Crumble (not for celiacs)

Serves 6

1 lb 10 oz	rhubarb, trimmed and chopped
2 tbsp	pear and apple all-fruit spread or sugar (raw cane)
2 oz	raisins
3 ½ fl oz	water
5 tbsp	oatmeal
1 tbsp	sesame seeds
1 tbsp	sunflower seeds

PER SERVING	
Calories	160.95
Protein g	4.32
Fat g	6.26
Saturated fatty acids g	1.91
MonounSaturated fatty acids g	2.99
PolyunSaturated fatty acids g	4.13
Carbohydrate g	23.42
Total Sugars g	16.56
Sodium mg	14.48
Fiber g	3.35

For anyone who finds kiwi fruit too sweet raw, cooking them even very lightly for a minute in the microwave brings out their sharpness amazingly.

Clean and cut up the rhubarb. Put it in a saucepan with the pear and apple spread, raisins and water. Bring gently to a boil and simmer for 5–10 minutes or until the rhubarb is nearly soft.

Transfer to a pie dish and drain off and reserve some of the juices if it looks too runny. Mix together the oatmeal, sesame and sunflower seeds and sprinkle them over the top of the rhubarb. Bake in a moderate oven (350°F) for 15–20 minutes or until the topping is lightly browned. Serve with the extra juice and cream, yogurt or ice cream.

Baked Fruit Tart

Serves 4

You may use any combination of fruit you chose in this dessert, but make sure that they have good, sharp flavors. Mandarin-orange sections, for example, might be rather bland.

2 oz	rice flour
3 oz	sifted garbanzo (garbanzo/fava bean) flour
2 oz	margarine
3 tbsp	water
1 tbsp	apple and pear all-fruit spread
1	cooking apple
1	large orange
2	kiwi fruit
4 ½ oz	creamy yogurt
1 oz	browned, flaked almonds

Heat the oven to 350°F.

Rub the margarine into the flours, then add enough water to make a soft dough. Roll out the pastry carefully and line a 6-inch round or oval pie dish. Line with foil or waxed paper and weight with beans. Bake for 10 minutes, then remove the foil and beans and return to the oven for another 10 minutes to crisp the pastry.

Smooth the pear and apple spread over the bottom of the dish.

Peel and slice the apple and lay it over the concentrate. Peel and thinly slice the orange and lay it over the apple, then do the same with the kiwi fruit. Cover with foil and bake in the oven for a further

PER SERVING	
Calories	287.94
Protein g	9.61
Fat g	12.82
Saturated fatty acids g	4.29
MonounSaturated fatty acids g	6.34
PolyunSaturated fatty acids g	3.34
Carbohydrate g	34.66
Total Sugars g	15.55
Sodium mg	117.31
Fiber g	4.76

If you allow the layer to get cold, you can cut it into rectangles or wedges and eat it like a flapjack.

PER SERVING	
Calories	221.8
Protein g	5.35
Fat g	7.69
Saturated fatty acids g	1.78
MonounSaturated fatty acids g	2.35
PolyunSaturated fatty acids g	1.33
Carbohydrate g	34.64
Total Sugars g	9.09
Sodium mg	92.88
Fiber g	4.38

20 minutes. Remove from the oven, allow to cool slightly then spread the yogurt over the fruit and sprinkle with the flaked almonds. Serve warm or at room temperature.

Oat and Raspberry Crumble
(not for celiacs)

Serves 6

If you cannot eats oats you should give this recipe a pass. For those who can it is a quite delicious mixture of chewy oats and succulent raspberries.

5 oz	oatmeal
2 oz	rice flour
2 oz	apple or apple and pear all-fruit spread
3 oz	margarine
7 oz	raspberries
7 oz	blackberries
4 oz	red currants
2 hpg tsp	arrowroot

Heat the oven to 350°F.

Mix the oatmeal and rice flour with the pear and apple spread and the margarine.

Purée half the fruit and chop the rest roughly.

Put the arrowroot in a small pan and add a little of the purée, stir until smooth, then add the rest of the purée.

Heat gently until the sauce thickens then amalgamate it with the chopped fruit. Spread half of the crumble mixture over the bottom of a shallow baking dish or pie dish—you need it to be at least ½ inch thick. Spread the fruit mixture over the crumble and the rest of the crumble over the fruit.

Bake for 30 minutes. Serve warm or cold, alone or with yogurt, cream or ice cream.

Sweet omelettes are greatly underused. If you do not like rum, or you are feeding it to children, substitute water for the rum and fill the omelette with a jam of your choice.

Sweet Rum Omelette

Serves 6

A great Victorian favorite, this omelette is quick to make and delicious.

6	medium eggs
6 tbsp	dark rum
3 oz	sugar (raw cane)
2 tbsp	sunflower oil

Whisk the eggs very thoroughly in a bowl with 2 oz of the sugar and 3 tablespoons of the rum—you want a generally frothy mixture. Heat the omelette pan with a little butter or sunflower oil until it is very hot, pour in the omelette mixture and cook as for an ordinary omelette. If you are doing two small omelettes, it would be better to cook them both at the same time, then turn them out onto the serving dish. Sprinkle them with the remaining sugar, warm the remaining rum, light it and pour it over the omelettes as they are carried to the table. If you are making one big omelette, you will have to put the pan under a hot broiler to finish the top; then sprinkle the sugar and lighted rum over the omelette in the pan and serve it straight to the table.

PER SERVING	
Calories	211.70
Protein g	7.71
Fat g	11.48
Saturated fatty acids g	2.46
MonounSaturated fatty acids g	3.85
PolyunSaturated fatty acids g	3.89
Carbohydrate g	13.41
Total Sugars g	13.41
Sodium mg	88.08
Fiber g	0.00

When pears are out of season you could substitute a 14 oz can of pineapple chunks, well drained.

Upside Down Ginger and Pear Cake

Serves 8

This dessert tastes especially good as it is sweetened entirely by dried fruit with their rich and complex flavors.

2 oz	candied ginger
4 oz	dates, dried
1	large banana
5 oz	butter or margarine
½ tsp	nutmeg
½ tsp	ground cinnamon
1 tsp	ground ginger
3	eggs
6 oz	garbanzo (garbanzo/fava bean) flour
1 lb 2 oz	pears

Heat the oven to 350°F.

Soak the ginger in boiling water for 15 minutes to remove most of the sugar, then rinse and chop it finely.

Pureé the dates with the banana in a food processor, transfer to a mixer, add the butter and beat until relatively light and fluffy. Add the spices then slowly beat in the eggs, adding a spoonful of flour with each one. Remove from the mixer and fold in the rest of the flour. If the mixture is dry, add a little milk or apple juice.

Spoon a thin layer of the cake mix over the bottom of a well-greased 8-inch pan—round or square as you choose. Peel and core the pears and lay them, in a pattern, rounded side down, over the mixture. Carefully spoon in the rest of the cake mix and smooth off the top.

Bake for 30–35 minutes or until a toothpick comes out clean. Invert onto a warmed serving dish and serve with yogurt or ice cream.

PER SERVING	
Calories	244.19
Protein g	9.03
Fat g	11.41
Saturated fatty acids g	3.61
MonounSaturated fatty acids g	5.37
PolyunSaturated fatty acids g	3.49
Carbohydrate g	28.43
Total Sugars g	17.56
Sodium mg	165.92
Fiber g	4.30

Baking: Cookies, Cakes and Breads

Macaroons

Cheese Scones

Chocolate Brownies

Blueberry and Cranberry Muffins

Passion Cake

Chocolate Puffs

Lemon Shortcakes

Chocolate Cake

Apple and Cinnamon Cake

Madeira Cake

Gooey Gingercake

Oatcakes (not for celiacs)

Banana Bread

Fruit Malt Loaf (not for celiacs)

Ginger Cake

Walnut and Coffee Sponge

Aunt Vi's Ginger Cookies

Light Sponge (Angel) Cake

Sponge Cake

Lemon Polenta Cake with Sunflower Seeds

Crispy Cookies (not for celiacs)

Light Fruit Cake

Yorkshire Pudding

Oaten Soda Bread (not for celiacs)

Rice and Corn Soda Bread

Wholemeal Loaf

Wholemeal Bread with Pine Nuts and Walnuts (not for celiacs unless they exclude the oats)

Stollen Bread

Golden Yeast Loaf

White Rice Loaf

Like meringues, you can also spread out the macaroon mix flat on rice paper on a baking sheet and use it as the base for a dessert.

Macaroons

Serves 20

If your macaroons go flat (which they often do!) they are excellent broken up as a topping for ice cream !

7 oz	ground almonds
7/8 cup	superfine sugar
3	egg whites
1 oz	arrowroot
2	drops vanilla extract
8	split almonds
	rice paper

Heat the oven to 350°F.

Beat together the ground almonds, sugar, egg whites, arrowroot and vanilla until they are very well amalgamated. If they seem runny, add a little extra ground almond. Line a baking sheet with rice paper cut to size.

Use a teaspoon to put 8 macaroons on the rice paper (if you have extra, make additional macaroons) and press a split almond into the top of each.

Bake the macaroons for approximately 10 minutes or until they are lightly tanned and crisp on the outside.

Cool completely before storing in a tin.

PER SERVING	
Calories	263.63
Protein g	6.02
Fat g	11.66
Saturated fatty acids g	1.12
MonounSaturated fatty acids g	7.25
PolyunSaturated fatty acids g	3.08
Carbohydrate g	36.74
Total Sugars g	33.85
Sodium mg	33.08
Fiber g	1.53

If you want to make the scones really cheesy, grate some extra cheese on top before you put them in the oven.

Cheese Scones

Serves 6

These scones are good when fresh but do not keep very well—so eat them on the day they are made.

2 oz	sifted garbanzo (garbanzo/fava bean) flour
3 oz	rice flour
	salt
1 hpg tsp	wheat- and gluten-free baking powder
3 oz	Cheddar cheese, grated
1 oz	margarine
5–6 tbsp	milk
1 tbsp	squeezed-fresh lemon juice

Preheat the oven to 400°F.

Mix the dry ingredients and cheese together, then rub in the margarine as though for pastry. Sour the milk with a squeeze of lemon juice, then mix it into the dry ingredients to make a moist dough.

Knead the dough lightly on a floured board and then press it out to approximately 1½ inches thickness. Cut out rounds (with a pastry cutter or a glass) or triangles.

Lay the scones on a floured baking sheet and bake them in a hot oven for 7–15 minutes, depending on how large you have made them. They should be lightly tanned but not burned. Cool on a rack.

PER SERVING	
Calories	151.57
Protein g	6.44
Fat g	7.22
Saturated fatty acids g	3.65
MonounSaturated fatty acids g	2.21
PolyunSaturated fatty acids g	0.85
Carbohydrate g	15.21
Total Sugars g	1.10
Sodium mg	247.65
Fiber g	1.14

Children may prefer the
brownies without the walnuts.

Chocolate Brownies

Makes 12 brownies

A good rich brownie recipe. If you are celiac and cannot eat oats
use 3 ½ oz of garbanzo flour instead of 2 and leave out the
oatmeal. The texture will not be as interesting but they will still
taste good.

5 oz	margarine
5 oz	sugar (raw cane)
2 oz	cocoa powder
2 oz	oatmeal, processed in a food processor to a coarse powder
2 oz	sifted garbanzo (garbanzo/fava bean) flour
2 oz	buckwheat flour
3 tsp	wheat- and gluten-free baking powder
5 fl oz	milk
2 oz	broken walnuts

Preheat the oven to 325°F.

With an electric mixer, beat the spread thoroughly with the sugar
and the cocoa.

Fold in the oatmeal, the flours and baking powder alternately
with the milk, and then fold in the walnuts.

Spoon the mixture into a well-oiled square (6 inch x 6 inch) or
rectangular baking pan, smooth out with a spatula and bake for 30
minutes or until a toothpick comes out clean.

Cool for a few minutes in the pan, then cut into whatever size
brownies you fancy.

Remove them carefully from the pan with a spatula and cool
on a rack.

EACH BROWNIE:	
Calories	189.65
Protein g	4.22
Fat g	9.96
Saturated fatty acids g	2.49
MonounSaturated fatty acids g	3.20
PolyunSaturated fatty acids g	3.37
Carbohydrate g	22.77
Total Sugars g	13.65
Sodium mg	193.92
Fiber g	1.47

If you cannot find fresh blueberries or cranberries, you could use plump raisins or even chocolate kisses.

Blueberry and Cranberry Muffins

Serves 6

Delicious for a lazy Sunday morning breakfast with the papers.

3 oz	margarine
1 ½ oz	sugar (raw cane)
1	small egg
4 fl oz	milk
3 oz	sifted garbanzo (garbanzo/fava bean) flour
3 oz	rice flour
1 hpg tsp	wheat- and gluten-free baking powder
	small pinch salt
½ tsp	vanilla extract
1 ½ oz	cranberries
1 ½ oz	blueberries

Heat the oven to 350°F.

Beat the margarine, sugar, egg and milk together with an electric mixer.

Mix the flours with the baking powder and salt and gradually beat them into the liquid mixture. Fold in the vanilla, cranberries and blueberries and spoon the dough into 6 greased pie or tart pans. Bake the muffins for 20 minutes or until they have risen and are firm to the touch. Remove them and cool slightly on a rack. The muffins are also good cold and freeze well.

PER SERVING	
Calories	187.02
Protein g	5.77
Fat g	7.54
Saturated fatty acids g	2.33
MonounSaturated fatty acids g	3.02
PolyunSaturated fatty acids g	1.77
Carbohydrate g	24.95
Total Sugars g	8.88
Sodium mg	235.57
Fiber g	1.91

Passion Cake

Serves 10

This passion cake is sweetened only by fruit, which adds to its flavor without making it too sweet.

3	medium eggs
4 oz	dried, pitted dates, (soaked in boiling water if they are very hard,) chopped
4 oz	margarine
5 oz	carrots, grated
5 oz	ripe pears, peeled, cored and puréed in a food processor
5 oz	garbanzo (garbanzo/fava bean) flour
2 hpg tsp	gluten-free baking powder
2 level tsp	ground cinnamon
1 level tsp	ground nutmeg
½ level tsp	ground allspice
	pinch salt
7 oz	plain cream cheese
2 tbsp	pear and apple all-fruit spread
1	grated rind of 1 orange

Preheat the oven to 375°F.

Whizz the eggs, dates and margarine together in a processor until they are creamy. Mix in the carrots and pears. Sift together the flour, baking powder and spices, then fold them into the liquid mixture, making sure they are thoroughly amalgamated. Pour into a buttered and floured 8-inch cake pan, with a removable bottom, and bake in a moderately hot oven for 25 minutes or until the cake is firm to the touch. Remove from the oven and allow to cool on a wire rack.

The cake can be eaten perfectly well as it is, but if you want to ice it, heat the pear and apple spread until it is just runny and mix it into the cream cheese along with the orange rind. Spread over the cake and allow to cool.

PER SERVING	
Calories	180
Protein g	7.7
Fat g	8.6
Saturated fatty acids g	2.8
MonounSaturated fatty acids g	3.5
PolyunSaturated fatty acids g	12
Carbohydrate g	20
Total Sugars g	12.6
Sodium mg	220
Fiber g	2.7

If you have a piping bag you can have great fun piping meringue into all kinds of shapes—animals, hearts, golf clubs—anything you want. Just be very careful, especially if you have thin pieces like legs, when you take them off the foil that they do not break.

Chocolate Puffs

Makes 20 puffs

These are delightful little chocolate meringues—excellent on their own or as an accompaniment to a dessert.

1	large egg white
4 oz	superfine sugar
1 oz	dark chocolate, grated

Beat the egg white until very stiff. Then beat in the sugar and grated chocolate; the mixture will go rather runny in the process but it does not matter. Line a baking sheet with foil. Grease the foil and drop very small teaspoonfuls of the mixture onto it, allowing a certain amount of room for each puff to spread. You should get around 20 puffs from the mixture.

Bake the puffs in a cool oven (225°F) for 1 hour or until they are completely dried out. Gently pry them off the foil and store in an airtight box ready for use.

PER PUFF	
Calories	53.97
Protein g	0.58
Fat g	0.77
Saturated fatty acids g	0.46
MonounSaturated fatty acids g	0.27
PolyunSaturated fatty acids g	0.07
Carbohydrate g	12.16
Total Sugars g	12.03
Sodium mg	8.38
Fiber g	0.00

You could use this shortcake as a base for strawberry shortcake. Just mix fresh strawberries into some lightly whipped and sweetened cream and pile them on top.

Lemon Shortcakes

Makes about 12, 1 per serving

These shortcakes are crumblier than those made with wheat flour so need careful handling—but they do taste excellent.

2 oz	butter
3 oz	sugar (raw cane)
	grated rind of 1 lemon
2 oz	ground almonds
4 oz	sifted garbanzo (garbanzo/fava bean) flour

Beat the butter with the sugar with an electric mixer until soft and light. Add the lemon rind, then rub in the ground almonds and flour with your fingers, working as lightly as you can. Pat the mixture into the bottom of a greased baking pan or shape it into a round approximately ½ inch thick. Bake in a moderate oven (325°F) for 15 minutes.

Remove and score (it should make around 12 shortcakes) with a knife; then return to the oven for another 5 minutes. Cool slightly, then cut along the score marks, remove carefully, with a spatula, to a rack and allow to get quite cold before serving.

PER SERVING	
Calories	106.85
Protein g	2.62
Fat g	6.18
Saturated fatty acids g	2.49
MonounSaturated fatty acids g	2.36
PolyunSaturated fatty acids g	0.93
Carbohydrate g	11.02
Total Sugars g	6.92
Sodium mg	35.88
Fiber g	1.20

You could also use this mixture to make individual chocolate cupcakes, but you would need to reduce the cooking time to around 15 minutes.

Chocolate Cake

Serves 10

A classic chocolate cake—a great favorite with children. It usually gets eaten before it gets a chance to get iced, but if you wish to ice it you can with a standard chocolate butter icing or just with melted chocolate, milk or plain.

5 oz	margarine or butter
6 oz	sugar (raw cane)
2 oz	cocoa powder
3 ½ fl oz	boiling water
3	medium eggs
5 oz	rice flour, brown if possible
2 hpg tsp	wheat- and gluten-free baking powder

Heat the oven to 350°F.

With an electric mixer, beat the margarine or butter with the sugar until light and fluffy. Meanwhile, mix the cocoa powder with the boiling water until you have a smooth paste. Beat the cocoa into the mixture, then slowly beat in the three eggs, each accompanied by a spoonful of flour. Fold in the rest of the flour mixed with the baking powder.

Pour the mixture into a well-greased 6- or 8-inch round cake pan with a removable bottom and bake for 30 minutes or until it is firm to the touch and a toothpick comes out clean from the middle. Cool slightly, then turn onto a rack to get cold before cutting.

PER SERVING	
Calories	271
Protein g	4.2
Fat g	15.4
Saturated fatty acids g	6.6
MonounSaturated fatty acids g	6.1
PolyunSaturated fatty acids g	1.6
Carbohydrate g	30.5
Total Sugars g	17.6
Sodium mg	317
Fiber g	0.9

This cake keeps excellently either in a container or in the fridge.

Apple and Cinnamon Cake

Serves 10

A delicious moist and spicy light fruitcake.

4 oz	margarine
7 oz	dried dates, finely chopped
8 oz	tart eating apples, cored, peeled and grated
2 hpg tsp	ground cinnamon
1 level tsp	ground mixed spice
	pinch salt
3 oz	raisins
2	medium eggs, beaten
6 fl oz	milk
4 oz	rice flour
4 oz	sifted garbanzo (garbanzo/fava bean) flour
2 hpg tsp	baking powder

Preheat the oven to 350°F and grease and line an 8-inch square pan. Put margarine, dates, apple, cinnamon, mixed spice and salt into a processor and blend thoroughly. Fold in the raisins and eggs, alternately with the mixed flours and milk. When all are amalgamated, transfer them into the prepared pan.

Bake for 30–40 minutes until dark golden and firm to the touch. Test with a toothpick. Remove from the oven and allow to cool in the pan for 10–15 minutes before turning onto a wire rack to cool completely.

PER SERVING	
Calories	241
Protein g	6.9
Fat g	6.9
Saturated fatty acids g	2.2
MonounSaturated fatty acids g	2.9
PolyunSaturated fatty acids g	1.9
Carbohydrate g	39
Total Sugars g	22.5
Sodium mg	214
Fiber g	2.9

It is important to toss the cherries in the flour if you do not want them all to sink to the bottom of the cake. Or maybe you prefer a cake with a layer of cherries at the bottom !

Madeira Cake

Serves 8

Plain madeira cake is always a great favorite, whether served with a glass of madeira or a cup of tea! Adding the cherries might be appropriate for a more festive occasion.

7 oz	butter
6 oz	superfine sugar
	grated rind and juice of 1 lemon
	pinch ground cinnamon
3	medium eggs
4 oz	glacé cherries (optional)
3 oz	sifted garbanzo (garbanzo/fava bean) flour
3 ½ oz	rice flour
1 hpg tsp	wheat- and gluten-free baking powder
4	drops vanilla extract

Pre-heat the oven to 325°F.

Cream the butter with the sugar until they are light and fluffy. Add the lemon rind and the cinnamon. Beat in the eggs, one at a time, adding a little flour with each.

Toss the cherries (if you are using them) in the remains of the mixed flours and baking powder and fold them into the mixture along with the flours, vanilla extract and lemon juice. If the mixture is too thick, add a little milk.

Spoon the mixture into a greased, removable-bottomed or lined 7-inch pan and bake for 40–50 minutes or until a toothpick comes out clean.

Remove from the oven and turn out onto a rack to cool.

PER SERVING, INCLUDING CHERRIES:	
Calories	377
Protein g	6.1
Fat g	21
Saturated fatty acids g	12.75
MonounSaturated fatty acids g	5.6
PolyunSaturated fatty acids g	1.3
Carbohydrate g	43
Total Sugars g	29
Sodium mg	249
Fiber g	1.53

The gingerbread is even better served warm as a dessert with vanilla ice cream.

Gooey Gingercake

Serves 10

This is a seriously, wonderfully gooey cake, based on a recipe given to me many years ago by a colleague's Scottish mother—and in the original it was even sweeter and even gooier !

4 oz	butter
4 oz	sugar (raw cane)
10 ½ oz	black molasses
3	medium eggs
8 oz	brown rice flour
1 tsp	gluten- and wheat-free baking powder
1 tsp	ground ginger
1 hpg tsp	mixed spice
1 hpg tsp	cinnamon

Melt the butter, sugar and molasses together in a pan or microwave. Remove from the heat. Beat the eggs into the melted mixture followed by the flour, baking powder and spices. Pour it (the mixture will be very runny) into a greased loaf or cake pan (the size will depend on whether you want a small, deep cake or a larger, flatter one) and bake in a moderately cool oven (325°F) for 1 hour. Take out of the oven and the pan and cool on a rack. Serve it sliced, plain or buttered.

PER SERVING	
Calories	296
Protein g	4.1
Fat g	10.3
Saturated fatty acids g	6
MounounSaturated fatty acids g	2.8
PolyunSaturated fatty acids g	0.5
Carbohydrate g	48.7
Total Sugars g	30.6
Sodium mg	157
Fiber g	0.4

Oatcakes are very good for cocktail canapés as they do not go soggy, especially if you spread them with a thin layer of butter first.

Oatcakes (not for celiacs)

Makes around 12 large or 24 cocktail size oatcakes

Delicious with paté or cheese, but not, alas, for those who cannot eat oatmeal.

8 oz	medium oatmeal, or mixed fine, medium and pinhead
4 oz	garbanzo (garbanzo/fava bean) flour
	small pinch of salt
1 tsp	gluten- and wheat-free baking powder
3 oz	margarine or butter

Put the oatmeal in a bowl and sift in the flour, salt and baking powder. Rub the margarine in as for pastry and mix to a stiff dough with cold water.

Turn the mixture onto a board sprinkled with oatmeal. Knead the dough lightly, roll it out thinly and cut it into rounds with a glass or pastry cutter. Make the cakes whatever size you want according to their purpose—for cheese crackers, cocktail snacks, etc. Place them on a lightly oiled baking sheet and bake in a moderate oven (350°F) for 20–25 minutes, but keep an eye on them to make sure they do not burn.

Cool on a rack and store in an airtight container or the freezer.

PER LARGE OATCAKE:	
Calories	125.92
Protein g	4.34
Fat g	4.61
Saturated fatty acids g	0.74
MonounSaturated fatty acids g	1.19
PolyunSaturated fatty acids g	0.84
Carbohydrate g	17.88
Total Sugars g	0.44
Sodium mg	102.10
Fiber g	2.17

You can eat the bread on its own or with butter. Real banana fans use it for banana sandwiches.

Banana Bread

Serves 8

A wonderful way to use up those over-ripe bananas that no one will eat.

4 oz	margarine
2	medium eggs
3 tbsp	milk
8 oz	garbanzo (garbanzo/fava bean) flour, sifted
1 tsp	baking soda
3	large, very ripe bananas

Preheat the oven to 350°F.

Beat the margarine with the eggs and milk until they are pale and fluffy. Sift the flour with the baking soda and add it alternately with the egg mixture. Mash the bananas and add them to the mixture with extra milk if it is too stiff. Spoon the mixture into a greased 1-lb loaf pan and bake in a moderate oven for 1–1½ hours or until a toothpick comes out clean. Cool on a rack.

PER SERVING	
Calories	195
Protein g	8.6
Fat g	8.33
Saturated fatty acids g	2
MonounSaturated fatty acids g	3.83
PolyunSaturated fatty acids g	2.3
Carbohydrate g	23
Total Sugars g	9
Sodium mg	189
Fiber g	3.4

Fruit breads like this keep very well and are great to carry as a snack in your pocket or bag.

Fruit Malt Loaf (not for celiacs)

Serves 8

Another old-fashioned recipe dating from the days when everyone had their spoonful of malt at breakfast time. You can still get it in delicatessens, health food stores and the occasional supermarket.

9 oz	garbanzo (garbanzo/fava bean) flour
2 hpg tsp	gluten-free baking powder
3 oz	black raisins
3 oz	golden raisins
1 tbsp	malt extract
9 fl oz	fat-free (skimmed) milk

Preheat the oven 325°F.

Sift the flour with the baking powder and mix in the fruit.

Heat the malt extract with the milk in a pan or a microwave and stir them into the dry mixture. Spoon the dough into a well-greased 1-lb loaf pan and bake for about 45 minutes or until a toothpick comes out clean.

Cool on a rack and eat alone or with a spread.

PER SERVING	
Calories	175
Protein g	7.6
Fat g	3
Saturated fatty acids g	0.9
MonounSaturated fatty acids g	0.7
PolyunSaturated fatty acids g	0.9
Carbohydrate g	31.5
Total Sugars g	16.4
Sodium mg	126
Fiber g	3.74

If you are only a moderate ginger enthusiast, you could leave out the stem ginger pieces and substitute 1 heaping teaspoon of ground ginger.

Ginger Cake

Serves 10

A rich ginger cake with delicious lumps of stem ginger for real ginger enthusiasts.

4 oz	margarine
2 oz	sugar (raw cane)
4 oz	maple syrup
3	medium eggs
4 ½ oz	buckwheat flour
4 oz	rice flour
2 hpg tsp	ground ginger
1 hpg tsp	ground cinnamon
1 tsp	ground nutmeg
2 oz	stem ginger pieces, chopped
4 fl oz	apple juice, unsweetened

Beat the margarine with the sugar until soft and light. Beat in the maple syrup, then slowly beat in the 3 eggs alternately with the buckwheat flour. Fold in the rice flour, spices and ginger pieces along with enough apple juice to keep the mixture moist. Spoon it into a 6- or 8-inch greased round cake pan, and bake for 35–40 minutes in a moderate oven (350°F) or until a toothpick comes out clean. Turn out of the pan and cool on a rack.

PER SERVING	
Calories	199
Protein g	4.6
Fat g	6.4
Saturated fatty acids g	1.9
MonounSaturated fatty acids g	2.8
PolyunSaturated fatty acids g	1.3
Carbohydrate g	32.3
Total Sugars g	12.6
Sodium mg	94
Fiber g	0.56

If you wished you could cover the cake with a caramel butter icing, but I feel that it is quite rich enough the way it is.

Walnut and Coffee Sponge

Serves 10

This cake tastes excellent with its large pieces of walnut—and it keeps very well in a tightly fitting container or covered with plastic wrap.

5 oz	butter or margarine
5 oz	sugar (raw cane)
3	medium eggs
5 oz	garbanzo (garbanzo/fava bean) flour
5 oz	rice flour
1 tsp	ground nutmeg
1 tsp	ground cinnamon
½ tsp	ground cloves
	small pinch of salt
2 hpg tsp	gluten- and wheat-free baking powder
½ pint	strong black coffee
5 oz	chopped walnuts

Heat the oven to 350°F.

Beat the butter with the sugar until it is fairly light and fluffy. Separate the eggs and beat the 3 egg yolks into the mixture.

Sift the flours with the spices, salt and baking powder, then add them to the butter and sugar mixture alternately with the coffee. Stir in the chopped walnuts. Whisk the egg whites until they hold their shape but are not stiff or dry and mix and fold them carefully into the cake mixture. Spoon all into an 8-inch round cake pan—or a similar capacity loaf pan—with a removable bottom or lined with waxed paper.

Bake for 50–60 minutes or until a toothpick comes out clean. Remove from the oven and the pan and cool on a rack.

PER SERVING	
Calories	398
Protein g	8.5
Fat g	25.8
Saturated fatty acids g	9.9
MonounSaturated fatty acids g	6.1
PolyunSaturated fatty acids g	8.4
Carbohydrate g	35.8
Total Sugars g	16.3
Sodium mg	260
Fiber g	2.4

These are particularly delicious served with a stewed fruit such as rhubarb.

Aunt Vi's Ginger Cookies

Makes around 12 cookies

As with all cookies free of wheat flour, these are pretty crumbly so need to be treated with care. But they are delicious and worth the effort !

1 ½ oz	sugar (raw cane)
2 oz	rice flour
1 ½ oz	garbanzo (garbanzo/fava bean) flour
2 tsp	ground ginger
	pinch of salt
3 oz	butter

Mix the sugar, flours, ginger and salt in a bowl and then rub in the butter—you can use a pastry mixer for this. Press the mixture out into a greased baking pan about ½ inch thick, and bake it for 10 minutes in a moderately hot oven (325°F). Take the tray out and cut the mixture into cookie shapes—return to the oven for a further 5 minutes or until the cookies are golden. Remove from the oven and allow to cool. They can be dusted with sifted powdered sugar or a little sprinkling of ground ginger.

PER COOKIE	
Calories	87.94
Protein g	1.04
Fat g	5.34
Saturated fatty acids g	3.40
Monounsaturated fatty g	1.28
PolyunSaturated fatty acids g	0.26
Carbohydrate g	9.35
Total Sugars g	3.61
Sodium mg	81.98
Fiber g	0.46

Light Sponge (Angel) Cake

Serves 10

This is excellent on its own just sprinkled with a little powdered sugar and layered with jam, but it also makes a first-class base for a wide range of desserts.

6	medium eggs
5 oz	superfine sugar
5 oz	rice flour

Heat the oven to 325°F.

Line a removable-bottomed 8-inch cake pan with lightly floured waxed paper.

Whisk the eggs and sugar together with an electric mixer until they are light and fluffy. Sift the flour into the bowl and fold it very carefully into the egg mixture making sure that you do not get any lumps of flour.

Pour the mixture into the pan and bake for 20–30 minutes or until the cake is firm to the touch.

Remove from the oven and, carefully, from the pan. Peel off the waxed paper and allow to cool on a rack.

If you are to use the cake in another recipe (trifle or tiramisu) and do not want to use it all, the leftover will freeze well.

PER SERVING	
Calories	66.9
Protein g	5.6
Fat g	4
Saturated fatty acids g	1.1
MonounSaturated fatty acids g	1.7
PolyunSaturated fatty acids g	0.4
Carbohydrate g	28.1
Total Sugars g	16
Sodium mg	52
Fiber g	0.3

Sponge Cake

Serves 10

This substantial but still excellent cake can be eaten on its own or used as a base for other dishes.

7 oz	butter
7 oz	sugar (raw cane)
3	medium eggs
7 oz	sifted garbanzo (garbanzo/fava bean) flour
2 tsp	gluten- and wheat-free baking powder
1 tsp	vanilla extract

Heat the oven to 350°F.

Beat the butter with the sugar until light and fluffy. Beating slowly, add the eggs alternately with the flour. Fold in the remaining flour, baking powder and vanilla. Spoon into a well-oiled or lined 8-inch pan, and bake for 30 minutes or until the cake is firm to the touch and a toothpick comes out clean. Cool on a rack and when cold, split and fill with jam of your choice. If you wish you can also dust the top with powdered sugar.

PER SERVING	
Calories	309
Protein g	6.3
Fat g	19.4
Saturated fatty acids g	11.4
MonounSaturated fatty acids g	5
PolyunSaturated fatty acids g	1.2
Carbohydrate g	30.6
Total Sugars g	21
Sodium mg	224
Fiber g	2.1

If you would rather have a totally smooth cake, leave out the sunflower seeds.

Lemon Polenta Cake with Sunflower Seeds

Serves 10

The lemon juice makes this a deliciously refreshing cake with morning coffee or afternoon tea.

2 oz	sunflower seeds
5 oz	butter
5 oz	sugar (raw cane)
2	whole eggs
2	egg yolks
4 oz	corn flour or polenta
3 oz	potato flour
2 hpg tsp	gluten- and wheat-free baking powder
	grated rind and juice of 2 lemons
3 tbsp	sweet white wine

Heat the oven to 350°F.

Pulse the sunflower seeds in a food processor until they are well broken but not powdered. Toast them lightly in a dry pan until they tan but do not let them burn. Cool.

Cream the butter with the sugar until light and fluffy. Add the eggs and egg yolks alternately with spoonfuls of the combined flours, beating slowly. By hand, fold in the rest of the flour and baking powder alternately with the lemon rind and juice, the sunflower seeds and the wine.

Spoon into a prepared 8-inch greased cake pan and bake for 30 minutes or until the cake is firm to the touch and a toothpick comes out clean.

Cool on a rack before cutting.

PER SERVING	
Calories	267
Protein g	5
Fat g	15.6
Saturated fatty acids g	7.7
MonounSaturated fatty acids g	4.3
PolyunSaturated fatty acids g	2.2
Carbohydrate g	28
Total Sugars g	14
Sodium mg	180
Fiber g	0.7

Another excellent carry-out snack. They are not too sweet, but because of the seeds they are really sustaining.

Crispy Cookies (not for celiacs)

Makes around 20 cookies

This recipe makes rather crisp and less gooey cookies than normal but the texture does depend on the oats so would be on the forbidden list for anyone who cannot eat oats.

4 oz	margarine
2 oz	sugar (raw cane)
2 oz	pancake syrup
8 oz	oatmeal
2 oz	pine nuts or sunflower seeds or a combination of the two

Heat the oven to 350°F.

Dissolve the margarine, sugar and syrup in a pan or microwave but do not let them boil or the cookies will get sticky rather than crisp.

Stir in the oats, nuts or seeds and mix them all well together. With your fingers, press the mixture out in a thin layer in the bottom of a greased metal or Pyrex pie dish. Cook for 30 minutes (or for 3 1/2–4 minutes in a microwave on full power). As soon as they are cooked, score them and cool slightly. Remove from the pan and allow to cool on a rack.

PER COOKIE	
Calories	88.3
Protein g	2.04
Fat g	4.72
Saturated fatty acids g	0.65
MonounSaturated fatty acids g	1.38
PolyunSaturated fatty acids g	1.52
Carbohydrate g	12.82
Total Sugars g	4.74
Sodium mg	43.72
Englyst Fiber g	0.81

Light Fruit Cake

Serves 10

This is a real fruit cake since the only sweeteners it contains are dried fruits. It makes quite a crumbly mixture so allow it to cool completely in the pan before turning it out.

4 oz	margarine or butter
2 oz	dried dates, softened in hot water
1	medium banana
	rind and juice of 2 oranges
	rind and juice of 1 lemon
3 oz	raisins
2 oz	currants
1 oz	mixed peel
2 oz	glacé cherries, halved
4 oz	ground almonds
3 oz	garbanzo (garbanzo/fava bean) flour
2 oz	brown rice flour
3 tsp	gluten- and wheat-free baking powder
2 tsp	ground nutmeg

Heat the oven to 325°F. Line an 8-inch cake pan with oiled waxed paper.

Soften the margarine or butter, then beat until creamy. Chop the dates in a food processor, then add the banana and purée. Beat this mixture into the creamed spread or butter, and beat in the orange and lemon juice and rind.

Fold in the raisins and currants, mixed peel, glacé cherries and ground almonds. Fold in the flours, baking powder and nutmeg and mix well. If the mixture is too dry add a little milk or extra orange juice.

Spoon the mixture into the lined pan and bake for 50 minutes—1 hour or until a toothpick comes out clean.

PER SERVING

Calories	224
Protein g	5
Fat g	11.3
Saturated fatty acids g	2.1
MonounSaturated fatty acids g	5.9
PolyunSaturated fatty acids g	3
Carbohydrate g	27.6
Total Sugars g	19.6
Sodium mg	167
Fiber g	2.3

Yorkshire Pudding

Serves 6

The pudding can be served with roast beef as normal, or you can serve it by itself with gravy—or even as a dessert with jam !

2 oz	garbanzo (garbanzo/fava bean) flour
2 oz	rice flour
1	egg
	salt and black pepper
7 fl oz	milk
2 tbsp	sunflower oil

Heat the oven to 450°F.

Put the flours, egg and milk, with a pinch of salt and a grind of black pepper, in the food processor and combine thoroughly.

Pour a couple of drops of sunflower oil into the bottom of 12 individual pie pans or one flat baking dish. Put in the oven for a couple of minutes to heat until the oil is smoking. Pour the batter into the individual holders or into the dish and return it to the oven at once. Bake for 20 minutes or until the puddings are risen and golden.

Serve at once with beef, with gravy, or with jam !

PER SERVING	
Calories	140.43
Protein g	4.67
Fat g	8.03
Saturated fatty acids g	1.83
MounounSaturated fatty acids g	1.99
PolyunSaturated fatty acids g	3.55
Carbohydrate g	12.67
Total Sugars g	2.08
Sodium mg	102.71
Fiber g	1.06

Real soda bread should be made with buttermilk, which may be substituted for the milk. If you are using milk and want to achieve a more authentic taste, add a squeeze of lemon juice to the milk to curdle it.

Oaten Soda Bread

(not for celiacs)

Makes 1 loaf

The oats give this bread a very good flavor but it is crumbly—so beware.

6 oz	potato flour
6 oz	oatmeal, processed until very fine
6 oz	brown rice flour
2 tsp	cream of tartar
1 tsp	baking soda
1 tbsp	soy flour
1 tsp	sugar
3/4 tsp	salt
1 tbsp	butter
1	large egg
10 fl oz	milk

Heat the oven to 350°F.

Mix all the dry ingredients thoroughly together in a large mixing bowl, then rub in the butter. Mix in the egg, followed by the milk, making sure there are no lumps.

Grease or oil a 6-inch round cake or loaf pan and pour the mixture in. Bake for 35–40 minutes or until the bread is risen and a toothpick comes out clean. Remove from the oven and cool for a few minutes in the pan, covered with a dry tea cloth. Remove carefully onto a wire rack and cover with a tea cloth until it is quite cold before slicing.

This bread is good cold but crumbles a lot if you try to toast it.

PER LOAF:	
Calories	2096.85
Protein g	61.42
Fat g	49.75
Saturated fatty acids g	18.20
MonounSaturated fatty acids g	11.16
PolyunSaturated fatty acids g	3.90
Carbohydrate g	361.93
Total Sugars g	22.73
Sodium mg	3372.10
Fiber g	23.43

Rice and Corn Soda Bread

Makes 1 loaf

Another no-yeast bread that is quite dense in texture but very well flavored.

5 oz	potato flour
5 oz	rice flour
2 oz	buckwheat flour
4 oz	fine corn flour
3 tsp	soy flour
1 tsp	baking soda
2 tsp	cream of tartar
1 tsp	sugar
3/4 tsp	salt
1/2 tbsp	butter
1	large egg, beaten
9 fl oz	milk

Heat the oven to 350°F.

Mix the flours together in a mixing bowl, then mix in the other dry ingredients. Rub in the butter, then stir in the egg and the milk, making sure that they are all thoroughly amalgamated.

Grease or oil a 6-inch round cake pan or loaf pan and pour in the soda bread mixture. Or form into a circle on a greased baking sheet and cut a cross in the top. Bake in the center of the oven for 45–50 minutes or until a toothpick comes out clean.

Allow to cool slightly in the pan, covered with a tea cloth, then remove carefully onto rack. Cover with a tea cloth and allow to get completely cold before slicing.

PER LOAF:	
Calories	2181.1
Protein g	65.45
Fat g	48.55
Saturated fatty acids g	23.9
MonounSaturated fatty acids g	13.44
PolyunSaturated fatty acids g	2.97
Carbohydrate g	379.38
Total Sugars g	33.76
Sodium mg	3462.35
Englyst Fiber g	14.63

Wholemeal Loaf

Makes 1 loaf

This is similar in taste and texture to a fairly dense wholemeal wheat loaf. The sesame seeds give a little extra interest—assuming that you are able to eat them—but are quite dispensable.

12 oz	brown rice flour
2 oz	buckwheat flour
2 oz	potato flour
1 tsp	soy flour
½ tsp	salt
2 tsp	sugar
1 ½ tsp	cream of tartar
¼ tsp	baking soda
2 tsp	active dry yeast
½ tbsp	butter
1	medium egg, beaten
½ tbsp	sesame seeds (optional)
15 fl oz	warm water (5 oz boiling combined with 10 oz room temperature)

Heat oven to 350°F. Grease a 2-lb loaf pan or a round cake pan.

Mix all the dry ingredients (except the sesame seeds) thoroughly in a large mixing bowl. Rub in the butter, then stir in the egg and half the sesame seeds, if you are using them. Stir the water gradually into the dry mix. This will make an extremely runny mixture, but do not worry, it will firm up in the baking.

Warm the pan and then pour in the mixture. Sprinkle over the remaining sesame seeds and bake it in the center of the oven for 40 minutes or until it has risen and a toothpick comes out clean.

Cool in the pan for 5–10 minutes under a tea cloth, then carefully remove onto a rack. Cover with a tea cloth and leave until it is quite cold before cutting.

PER LOAF:	
Calories	2028.73
Protein g	44.25
Fat g	37.74
Saturated fatty acids g	14.16
MonounSaturated fatty acids g	11.22
PolyunSaturated fatty acids g	6.65
Carbohydrate g	373.48
Total Sugars g	13.48
Sodium mg	2326.4
Fiber g	13.16

Wholemeal Bread with Pine Nuts and Walnuts

(not for celiacs unless they exclude the oats)

Makes 1 loaf

A party version of the plain wholemeal loaf. Those who cannot eat oats can just leave them out.

10 oz	brown rice flour
4 oz	cornmeal
2 oz	buckwheat flour
1 tsp	soy flour
1 tbsp	oatmeal, pulverized in a food processor (optional)
1 scant tsp	salt
3 tsp	gluten- and wheat-free baking powder
2 tsp	sugar
½ tsp	active dry yeast
2 tsp	sesame seeds
1 tbsp	chopped walnuts
1 tbsp	pine nuts
1 tbsp	butter
1	egg, beaten
18 fl oz	warm water

Heat the oven to 350°F.

Mix all the dry ingredients well together then rub in the butter. Stir in the egg. Add 12 fl oz of cold water to 6 fl oz of boiling and mix it into the dry mix. You will end up with a very runny mix.

Grease or oil a 2-lb oblong or round loaf pan and pour in the mixture. Bake it in the center of the oven for 50–60 minutes or until a toothpick comes out clean. Cool for 5 minutes in the pan, covered with a tea cloth, then carefully remove and place on a rack. Cover with a tea cloth and allow to get completely cold before cutting.

PER LOAF:	
Calories	2444.28
Protein g	56.15
Fat g	70.58
Saturated fatty acids g	16.41
Monounsaturated fatty acids g	17.65
Polyunsaturated fatty acids g	24.24
Carbohydrate g	390.52
Total Sugars g	13.93
Sodium mg	3589.15
Fiber g	13.95

Stollen Bread

Makes 1 loaf

Although this calls itself a bread and is based on a bread recipe it is really more of a cake texture than a bread. Nonetheless, it tastes delicious!

10 oz	rice flour
2 oz	sugar
1/2 tsp	salt
1/2 tsp	active dry yeast
1 tsp	cream of tartar
1/2 tsp	baking soda
1 tbsp	ground almonds
2 tbsp	butter
1 tbsp	mixed peel
1 tbsp	glacé cherries, chopped
1 tbsp	raisins
	grated peel of 1 lemon
1 tbsp	sunflower seeds, chopped roughly
1 tbsp	pumpkin seeds, chopped roughly
1	medium egg, beaten
4 fl oz	warm, 1% milk

Heat the oven to 300°F.

In a large bowl, mix together the flour, salt, sugar, yeast, baking soda, cream of tartar and ground almonds. Rub in the butter, then add the other dry ingredients. Mix in the egg and then the warm milk.

Spoon the mixture into a well-greased 1-lb loaf or round cake pan and bake in the center of the oven for 30–35 minutes or until a toothpick comes out clean. Remove from the oven and allow to cool for a few minutes in the pan, before turning out carefully onto a rack. Cover with a tea cloth and allow to cool completely before cutting.

Serve alone or with butter or jam.

PER LOAF:	
Calories	2378.13
Protein g	50.72
Fat g	81.96
Saturated fatty acids g	25.34
MonounSaturated fatty acids g	27.62
PolyunSaturated fatty acids g	20.09
Carbohydrate g	358.52
Total Sugars g	109.74
Sodium mg	1580.40
Fiber g	12.60

Breads made with wheat flour have gluten to help hold them up once they have risen. Some breads made with rice flour may sink a little when cooked. They may not look as good but they are just as, if not more, delicious to eat.

Golden Yeast Loaf

Makes 1 loaf

This makes an excellent light golden-colored loaf with a good texture.

10 oz	rice flour
3 oz	corn flour
1 tsp	soy flour
½ tsp	salt
½ tbsp	active dry yeast
2 tsp	sugar
1 tsp	cream of tartar
½ tsp	baking soda
1 tbsp	butter
1	large egg, beaten
15 fl oz	warm water made up of ⅓ boiling water and ⅔ cold tap water

In a large bowl, mix all the dry ingredients together, then rub in the butter. Add the egg and water and stir well together to make a really sloppy mixture. Stir this very well (by hand, not in a mixer) until it is thoroughly amalgamated.

Grease and warm a 2-lb loaf pan and pour in the mixture. Cover it with greased aluminum foil and allow it to rise in a warm place for 20 minutes.

Heat the oven to 400°F.

Remove the foil and bake for 10 minutes in the hot oven. Reduce the heat to 350°F and continue to bake for a further 15 minutes by which time the loaf should have risen and a toothpick comes out clean.

Cool the loaf for some minutes in the pan, then carefully remove it onto a rack, cover with a cloth and allow to cool completely.

PER LOAF:

Calories	1678.43
Protein g	38.71
Fat g	28.16
Saturated fatty acids g	12.71
MonounSaturated fatty acids g	6.85
PolyunSaturated fatty acids g	1.42
Carbohydrate g	308.08
Total Sugars g	12.04
Sodium mg	1910.20
Fiber g	8.33

White Rice Loaf

Makes 1 loaf

The best texture is achieved by part microwaving the bread and then baking it, although it also works well (if you do not have a microwave) baking it in a bain marie (water bath).

10 oz	rice flour
1 tbsp	active dry yeast
1 tbsp	sugar
1 tsp	salt
9 fl oz	warm water made up of 1/3 boiling water and 2/3 cold tap water
2	medium eggs, beaten
2 tbsp	sunflower oil

Put the flour, yeast, sugar and salt in a mixing bowl, add the water and mix well. Add the egg and oil and mix again. Pour the mixture into very-well-oiled containers:

1. A 2 1/2-pint microwave container for the microwave version.

2. A 1-lb loaf pan for the oven version.

Both versions: Cover with well-oiled foil and allow to rise for 20 minutes in a very warm place.

To bake:

1. Microwave. Uncover the bread, place it in a microwave baking tray and bake on High for 6 minutes. Meanwhile, heat the oven to 450°F.

   Remove the bread from the microwave, allow to cool for a few minutes then turn out onto a baking sheet. Bake, uncovered for 10-15 minutes to give it a crust.

   Remove onto a baking rack, cover with a tea cloth and allow to cool.

2. Oven: Preheat the oven to 450°F. Place the risen dough in the loaf pan in a baking dish and pour boiling water into the baking dish up to half the loaf pan height. Bake, covered for 10 minutes. Reduce the heat to 350°F and bake for a further 20 minutes uncovered. Remove from the oven, allow to cool for a few minutes, then turn out onto a baking sheet. Increase the oven temperature again to 450°F and return the loaf to the oven, uncovered, for a further 10–15 minutes to allow it to form a crust.

Turn out carefully onto a wire rack and cover with a cloth to cool.

PER LOAF:	
Calories	1606.00
Protein g	38.80
Fat g	45.14
Saturated fatty acids g	7.22
MonounSaturated fatty acids g	11.80
PolyunSaturated fatty acids g	20.44
Carbohydrate g	152.50
Total Sugars g	11.94
Sodium mg	2122.56
Fiber g	6.00

Festive Feasts—
Easter and Christmas

Christmas Fruit Cake

Capon or Turkey Roasted in Honey

Chicken or Turkey Stuffing

Rice Sauce

Mince Pie

Pumpkin Pie

Christmas Pudding

This cake can be left exactly as it is or it can be iced with marzipan and white icing for Christmas. Since few families seem able to agree about icing on Christmas cakes, maybe you could just ice half of it and leave the other half untouched !

Christmas Fruit Cake

Serves 10

An excellent cake that keeps well. It should feed 10 people amply over the Christmas holiday.

3 oz	dried apricots, soaked for 30 minutes in boiling water if hard
3 oz	dried dates, soaked for 30 minutes in boiling water if hard
3 oz	dried prunes, soaked for 30 minutes in boiling water if hard
2 tbsp	brandy
	rind and juice of 2 lemons
3 oz	margarine or butter
2	medium eating apples, cored but not peeled and minced in a food processor
2	medium pears, cored but not peeled and minced in a food processor
4 1/2 oz	rice flour
4 1/2 oz	garbanzo (garbanzo/fava bean) flour
5 hpg tsp	gluten- and wheat-free baking powder
1 tsp	each ground ginger and ground cinnamon
2 oz	ground almonds
5 oz	black raisins
5 oz	golden raisins
5 oz	currants
2 oz	broken walnuts
5 tbsp	coconut milk or ordinary cow's milk

Heat the oven to 300°F. Grease a an 8-inch pan and line it with waxed paper.

Chop the apricots, dates and prunes by hand or in a food processor. Mix them with the brandy, lemon juice and rind and set aside.

PER SERVING	
Calories	375.81
Protein g	7.69
Fat g	10.46
Saturated fatty acids g	1.91
MonounSaturated fatty acids g	4.35
PolyunSaturated fatty acids g	4.60
Carbohydrate g	64.28
Total Sugars g	4.75
Sodium mg	261.73
Fiber g	5.24

Cream the margarine or butter with the minced apple and pear mixture and then beat in the dried fruits in their soaking liquid. Sieve together the flours, baking powder and spices. Fold them into the fruit mixture along with the ground almonds, raisins, currants, and walnuts. Add the milk as required to make a stiff but moist dough.

Spoon into the cake pan and bake, uncovered, for 2 hours or until a toothpick comes out of the middle clean.

Capon or Turkey Roasted in Honey

Enough to stuff a bird large enough to feed 10

A very dramatic old English recipe—great for Christmas or any other festive occasion.

about 5 lb	capon or small turkey
2 oz	the liver from the bird
3 oz	butter
1	medium onion, finely chopped
	large handful of parsley, finely chopped
3 oz	cooking apple, peeled and chopped small
3 oz	plump raisins
	rind and juice of 1 1/2 lemons
3 oz	ground almonds
3 oz	cooked white rice
1 tsp	ground ginger
1 tsp	salt
1/2 tsp	black pepper
1	egg
2 tbsp	honey

Remove the giblets from the bird, retain the liver and discard (or make stock from) the rest.

Melt 1 oz of the butter in a saucepan, add the onion, liver and parsley and fry gently until the onion is soft and the liver firm. Take off the heat and add the apple, raisins, lemon, almonds, cooked rice, seasoning and egg. Mix well.

Stuff the bird at both ends and secure with a skewer. Place in a roasting pan. Melt the honey with the rest of the butter and spoon the mixture over the bird; as it cools it will cling fairly well to the skin. Leave the bird to marinate in the honey in the refrigerator for 24 hours, spooning over any excess mixture every now and then.

To cook, heat the oven to 350°F. Roast the bird, uncovered, basting it frequently with the honey and butter mixture, for approximately 20 minutes per pound. The skin will gradually turn black and shiny in contrast to the very white meat underneath. Serve either warm or cold.

PER SERVING	
Calories	513.52
Protein g	35.32
Fat g	34.00
Saturated fatty acids g	11.21
MonounSaturated fatty acids g	15.18
PolyunSaturated fatty acids g	5.76
Carbohydrate g	17.29
Total Sugars g	10.82
Sodium mg	266.60
Fiber g	1.06

Chicken or Turkey Stuffing

Enough to stuff a bird large enough to feed 10

Millet is another cereal grain that is high in fiber but gluten free. It is a small, hard round grain which needs long cooking (excellent in a stuffing) and also is used as a flour in some proprietary wheat- and gluten-free flour mixes.

7 oz	whole millet grain
18 fl oz	water
2 tbsp	olive oil
10½ oz	onions, peeled and chopped finely
2	sticks celery, chopped small
1 oz	sun-dried tomatoes, chopped very small
6	bacon slices, chopped small
5½ oz	raw chicken liver, chopped
2 oz	whole cashew nuts
2	eggs
7 fl oz	medium sherry
	sea salt
	freshly ground black pepper

Put the millet grain in a large saucepan with the water, bring to a boil and simmer gently for 10 minutes. Turn off the heat, cover the pan and leave it to steam for a further 10 minutes. (Note: These instructions are for natural, untouched millet grain. Check on your pack; if it has already been processed it may need less cooking or less water.)

Meanwhile heat the oil in a large pan and add the onion, celery, sun-dried tomatoes and bacon slices. Cook briskly, without burning, for 5–10 minutes or until the vegetables are soft. Add the chicken liver and continue to cook for a further 3–4 minutes.

Take off the heat and add the nuts, eggs and sherry, then the millet. Mix very thoroughly, then season to taste.

The stuffing is now ready to go into the bird. If you have too much, make little balls out of what is leftover and roast them for 15–20 minutes in the roasting pan beside the bird.

PER SERVING	
Calories	294.66
Protein g	9.83
Fat g	17.29
Saturated fatty acids g	5.33
PolyunSaturated fatty acids g	2.60
MonounSaturated fatty acids g	8.67
Carbohydrate g	19.53
Total Sugars g	2.94
Sodium mg	398.52
Fiber g	0.75

Rice Sauce

Serves 6

Traditionally eaten with Christmas turkey.

4 oz	white rice
1½ pints	milk
1–2	medium onions stuck with around 12 whole cloves
	salt and 10 black peppercorns

Put the rice in a pan with the milk and the onions stuck with the cloves and the peppercorns. Bring slowly to a boil and simmer very gently, taking care it does not stick or burn, for 20–30 minutes or until the rice is quite soft. Remove the cloves from the onions and purée the milky rice in a food processor. Depending on how strong an onion flavor you like, purée the onions with the mixture or remove them first. Season to taste with salt and reheat gently in a pan or (better) in a microwave before serving.

PER SERVING	
Calories	123.63
Protein g	4.68
Fat g	4.48
Saturated fatty acids g	2.83
MonounSaturated fatty acids g	1.36
PolyunSaturated fatty acids g	0.13
Carbohydrate g	16.36
Total Sugars g	6.23
Sodium mg	62.25
Fiber g	0.18

Mince Pie

Serves 12

This mincemeat has no added sugar so although it is rich it is not as cloying as many mince pie mixtures.

13 oz	sifted garbanzo (garbanzo/fava bean) flour
1 oz	sugar (raw cane)
5 oz	dairy free margarine
8 oz	raisins
4 oz	currants
2 oz	glacé cherries
2 oz	mixed peel
1 tsp	ground ginger
1 tsp	ground nutmeg
½ tsp	ground mace
2 tsp	ground cinnamon
1	medium-sized, tart eating apple
1	orange
5 fl oz	brandy or whisky

Mix the sugar into the flour, then cut and rub in the margarine until it is well crumbled. Add about 12 tablespoons of cold water and mix to a dough. It needs to be pretty sticky if it is not to crumble. Use extra gram flour to dust a board, then roll out as normal.

Line a 9-inch pie dish with the pastry (if it tears just patch it with extra dough), line with foil, weight with beans and bake empty for 10 minutes in a moderate oven (350°F). Remove the beans and foil and continue to bake for a further 5 minutes, then cool.

Mix all the dry fruits with the spices.

Put the apple, cored and quartered but not peeled, and the orange, cut into quarters but not peeled, in a food processor and purée. Add this mixture to the dry fruit mixture, along with the brandy or whisky. Mix well, cover and set aside for 2–24 hours.

When ready to make the pie, mix the fruit mixture well together, then fill the pastry shell with it. Top the pies with a pastry lid or with a lattice work of pastry and decorate it as you feel inclined. You may also brush the top with egg.

Bake in a moderately hot oven (375°F) for approximately 15 minutes or until the crust is lightly tanned and crisp.

You can sprinkle the pie with sugar when it comes out of the oven.

PER SERVING	
Calories	432.93
Protein g	8.68
Fat g	19.03
Saturated fatty acids g	8.27
PolyunSaturated fatty acids g	3.44
MonounSaturated fatty acids g	7.08
Carbohydrate g	52.55
Total Sugars g	34.34
Sodium mg	162.40
Fiber g	5.42

Pumpkin Pie

Serves 8

Many cooks use ready-made pumpkin pie mix, but I have found that the improved taste so outweighs the extra effort in using fresh pumpkin that it is well worthwhile.

7 oz	sifted garbanzo (garbanzo/fava bean) flour
4 oz	butter
4 tbsp	water
12 oz	mashed pumpkin flesh—it is best to steam the pumpkin pieces and then mash the flesh like a potato
5 oz	coarse brown sugar
1 tbsp	black molasses
½ tsp	ground nutmeg
½ tsp	ground cinnamon
½ tsp	salt
2	eggs
4 fl oz	fresh heavy cream
2 oz	broken pecans

Ginger meringue topping—optional:

2	egg whites
2 oz	powdered sugar
1 tsp	lemon juice
2 oz	stem ginger, chopped

Heat the oven to 350°F.

Rub the butter into the flour, then mix to a soft dough with the water. Roll out the pastry and line an 8-inch pie dish. Line it with foil and weight it with beans or rice, then bake it empty for 10 minutes with the foil and beans, then another 10 minutes without.

Lower the oven to 325°F.

In a bowl, mix the pumpkin flesh with the sugar, molasses and spices. Whisk the eggs with the cream and add them to the

PER SERVING, INCLUDING THE MERINGUE TOPPING:	
Calories	405.53
Protein g	9.17
Fat g	25.05
Saturated fatty acids g	12.40
MonounSaturated fatty acids g	8.76
PolyunSaturated fatty acids g	3.12
Carbohydrate g	39.12
Total Sugars g	26.69
Sodium mg	202.29
Fiber g	3.41

pumpkin mixture, then stir in the nuts. Spoon the mixture into the pre-baked pie shell and cook for 45–50 minutes or until the custard is set.

Optional ginger meringue:

Whisk the egg whites with the powdered sugar and lemon juice until very stiff and shiny. Fold in the chopped ginger and spread the meringue mixture over the cooked pie. Return to a slightly hotter oven for 15–20 minutes just to set and color the meringue. Serve warm or cold.

Christmas Pudding

Serves 10

If any of the fruits seem rather hard, soak them for 10–15 minutes in boiling water before making the pudding. You can cook—or at least reheat—the pudding in the microwave, but it will not be as light.

4 oz	raisins
2 oz	currants
1 oz	mixed peel
1 oz	ready-to-eat prunes
1 oz	dried apricots
1 oz	dried dates
4 oz	tart eating apples, peeled, cored and chopped
½ tsp	ground ginger
½ tsp	ground cinnamon plus ¼ tsp ground mace
1 oz	flaked almonds
2 oz	garbanzo (garbanzo/fava bean) flour
2 oz	rice flour
2	eggs
4 tbsp	brandy or orange juice, or a combination of the two
3 tbsp	milk

Mix the fruits with the spices and the nuts. Sieve the garbanzo flour and add it to the fruit mixture with the rice flour. Beat the eggs with the brandy and the milk and stir it into the mixture. Spoon the mixture into an ovenproof pudding bowl, cover with doubled waxed paper and tie with a string or rubber bands. Put the bowl in a deep pan, pour in water to half way up the bowl, cover the pan tightly and simmer for 4–5 hours, checking periodically to make sure that the water has not dried up.

PER SERVING

Calories	174.05
Protein g	4.29
Fat g	5.56
Saturated fatty acids g	1.89
MonounSaturated fatty acids g	2.30
PolyunSaturated fatty acids g	1.00
Carbohydrate g	23.98
Total Sugars g	17.27
Sodium mg	36.38
Fiber g	1.87

Resources

Internet

General information: www.celiac.com—*A comprehensive website that addresses all aspects of the gluten-free diet and allows users to post messages on listservs with special topics, such as teens, parents, etc.*

National Institute of Health: www.niddk.nih.gov/health/digest/pubs/celiac/index.htm—*Includes articles on celiac disease, treatment, and the gluten-free diet.*

Listserv: listserv@maelstrom.stjohns.edu—*An international automatic mailing list that allows thousands of participants to share information about all aspects of living with celiac disease.*

Books

Case, Shelley: *Gluten-Free Diet: A Comprehensive Resource Guide.* Case Nutrition Consulting.

Korn, Danna: *Kids with Celiac Disease: A Family Guide to Raising Happy, Healthy, Gluten-Free Children.* Woodbine House.

Korn, Danna: *Wheat-Free, Worry-Free: The Art of Happy, Healthy, Gluten-Free Living.* Hay House.

Lowell, Jax Peters: *Against the Grain: The Slightly Eccentric Guide to Living Well Without Gluten or Wheat.* Henry Holt & Co.

Publications

Sully's Living Without, a magazine for people with food and chemical sensitivities. Go to www.livingwithout.com for subscription information.

Gluten-Free Living, a publication for people with celiac disease that discusses current issues and diet information. Write: P.O. Box 105, Hastings-on-Hudson, NY 10706 for subscription information.

National Celiac Disease Organizations

Celiac Disease Foundation
13251 Ventura Boulevard, Suite 1
Studio City, CA 91604-1838
Phone/ 818.990.2354
Website/ www.celiac.org

Celiac Sprue Association/U.S.A.
P.O. Box 31700
Omaha, NE 68131-0700
Phone/ 402.558.0600
Website/ www.csaceliacs.org

Friends of Celiac Disease Research
8832 North Port Washington Road #204
Milwaukee, WI 53217
Phone/ 414.540.6679
Website/ www.friendsofceliac.com

Gluten Intolerance Group
15110 10th Avenue S.W., Suite A
Seattle, WA 98166-1820
Phone/ 206.246.6652
Website/ www.gluten.net

R.O.C.K. (Raising Our Celiac Kids)
(chapters throughout the country)
3527 Fortuna Ranch Road
Encinitas, CA 92024
Phone/ 858.395.5421
Website/ www.celiackids.com

University of Chicago Celiac Disease Program
5841 South Maryland Avenue
MC 4065
Chicago, IL 60637
Phone/ 773.702.7593
Website/ www.celiacdisease.net

University of Maryland Celiac Research Center
22 South Greene Street, Box 140
Baltimore, MD 21201
Website/ www.celiaccenter.org

INDEX OF RECIPES

Satay, chicken, 70–1

Sauces: lemon w. lemon chicken in batter, 74–5; mushroom w. buckwheat pancakes, 127–8; orange & artichoke hearts w. turkey, 69–70; rice, 201; sunflower & cilantro pesto, 53; tomato for pasta, 55; tomato for pizza, 136–7; walnut w. steamed potatoes, 23

Sausage, bacon & apple pie, 17; cassoulet, 89–90; curried pasta &, 54; paella, 45; pork w. oatmeal, 99; pork w. polenta, 100

Scones: cheese, 167; crab cobbler, 43

Seafood see Fish; Shellfish

Seedy pastry squares, 19

Shellfish: Edward Abbott's salad, 39; paella, 45, see also Crab; Shrimp; Squid

Shortcakes, lemon, 172

Shrimp: Guyanan okra w., 42; paella, 45

Smoked fish see Fish

Soda bread: oaten, 189; rice & corn, 190

Soufflé, hot chocolate, 148

Soups: cream of mushroom, 13; creamed green pea w. pine nuts, 14; kidney, 15; leek, potato & smoked mackerel, 16; sweet potato w. coriander & ginger, 12

Spaghetti: bolognese, 61; w. smoked salmon, 57–8

Spinach: & artichoke pie, 126; eggs florentine, 24; green pie for

St. Patrick's Day, 124; vegetarian pasta w. fava beans &, 66

Sprouts, Brussels, stir-fried w. ginger, 135

Squid pilaff, Persian, 35

Steak & kidney pie, 88–9

Stir-fries: artichokes w. tuna, 47; Brussels sprouts w. ginger, 135; tofu & broccoli, 120

Stollen bread, 193

Stuffing for chicken or turkey, 200–1

Sunflower seed(s): & cilantro pesto, 53; lemon polenta cake w., 185; & mushroom pie, 117

Sweet & sour pork, 102–3

Sweet potato: & okra bake, 132; soup w. coriander & ginger, 12; & tomato bake, 116

Sweetcorn: & beef hash pie, 85; Mexican rice w. peppers &, 118; & tuna macaroni, 64

T

Tarts: baked fruit, 161–2; Bakewell, 154; carrot & ginger, 144

Terrine of chicken and walnuts, 21

Toast, French, 28

Tofu: & broccoli stir-fry, 120; & cranberry risotto, 121

Tomato(es): baked potatoes w. cheese &, 110; sauce for pasta, 55; sauce for pizza, 136–7; & sweet potato bake, 116

Trifle, 153–4

Tuna: & corn macaroni, 64; curry w. coconut & cilantro, 36; stir-fried artichokes w., 47

Turkey: w. artichoke hearts & orange sauce, 69–70; roasted in honey, 199–200; stuffing for, 200–1

V

Vegetable(s): crudités, 27; dahl, 137; pasta primavera, 59; pasta rusticana, 63; slow roasted w. artichokes, 123; winter casserole, 129, see also individual vegetables e.g. Carrots

Vermicelli & apple pudding, 151

Vol au vent shells, 29

W

Walnut(s): & coffee sponge cake, 181; sauce w. steamed potatoes, 23; terrine of chicken &, 21; wholemeal bread w. pine nuts &, 192

Wholemeal loaf, 191; w. pine nuts & walnuts, 192

Y

Yogurt, curried lamb w., 94

Yorkshire pudding, 188

Z

Zucchini: leg of lamb w. butter beans &, 97; salad of butter beans &, 133